POCKET
# FINANCE

# POCKET
# FINANCE

*The essentials of
the world of finance
from A to Z*

THE ECONOMIST IN ASSOCIATION WITH
HAMISH HAMILTON LTD
Published by the Penguin Group
Penguin Books Ltd, 27 Wrights Lane, London W8 5TZ, England
Penguin Books USA Inc., 375 Hudson Street, New York,
New York 10014, USA
Penguin Books Australia Ltd, Ringwood, Victoria, Australia
Penguin Books Canada Ltd, 10 Alcorn Avenue, Toronto,
Ontario, Canada M4V 3B2
Penguin Books (NZ) Ltd, 182–190 Wairau Road, Auckland 10,
New Zealand

Penguin Books Ltd, Registered Offices:
Harmondsworth, Middlesex, England

First published by Hamish Hamilton Ltd
in association with The Economist Books Ltd 1994

3 5 7 9 10 8 6 4

Copyright © The Economist Newspaper Ltd, 1994

**Chief contributor**  Tim Hindle

Printed and bound in Great Britain by
William Clowes Limited, Beccles and London

A CIP catalogue record for this book is available
from the British Library

ISBN 0-241-00241-9

# Contents

# INTRODUCTION

*Pocket Finance* is one in a new series of books that bring the clarity for which *The Economist* is famous to the often confusing subject of business. It is written by Tim Hindle, a former management editor of The Economist, and is divided into three parts.

Part 1 consists of essays which look at several of the most important features and issues concerning the way the financial world operates today.

Part 2 is an A–Z of terms which are widely used by those in finance and business but not always fully understood by those using them. Throughout this section are sprinkled lively quotations providing often witty insights, together with numerous nuggets of fact, many highlighting notable financial ups and downs.

In this section words in small capitals usually indicate a separate entry, thus enabling readers to find other relevant information (though they should note that abbreviations, such as EC and IBM, are also in small capitals).

Part 3 consists of numerous appendixes with information in the form of tabulated data, providing easy reference to a great variety of financial subjects.

The Pocket Management series is designed to take the mystique out of business and financial jargon in a stimulating and entertaining way. Other titles in the series include:

*Pocket MBA*
*Pocket Manager*
*Pocket Marketing*
*Pocket Negotiator*
*Pocket Strategy*

## Part 1

# ESSAYS

# TRACKING SAVINGS FROM THEIR SOURCE

Money, of course, makes the world go round. Nevertheless it is surprising that the allocation of it to different competing demands should occupy so many waking hours of some of the greatest minds on the planet. In the USA, Europe and Japan the brightest and most worldly young graduates are attracted by the idea of working in financial markets. There they find problem-solving galore (the staple diet of their education); much number-crunching in which to show off their numeracy skills; the prospect of ample foreign travel; like-minded workmates; and a salary that will never be mean, and may even be handsome.

All this, however, should not make them forget that finance and financial markets are only a means to an end. Bankers, stockbrokers and the like are merely conduits that pass money from an original saver to a final user. The conduits often try to make themselves seem more important than either the saver or the borrower, using devices like posh accents, dark suits and tall glass buildings to achieve their desired effect. But the truth is that only a few generations ago bankers were no more than moneylenders, and financial markets no more significant than a fish or a fur bazaar.

## In the beginning

All finance begins with saving, that is, somebody's decision to consume less now in order to be able to consume more later. In this sense financial institutions (like banks) are to money what the video-cassette recorder is to broadcasting: they enable consumers to time-shift their consumption.

Financial institutions bridge the gap between the time when people decide to save and the time when they decide to consume. Modern developed societies tend to save around 15–20% of their GNP, the total value of what they produce during the year. In other words, out of every $10 earned $1.50–2.00 goes into the bank.

In many modern societies there is a tendency

among ordinary folk to believe that saving is an unmitigated good, and consumption something to be done furtively and out of sight. This tendency was reversed somewhat in the 1980s when bold "conspicuous consumers" came out of the closet. But the "negative nineties" have brought back the idea that diligent saving is the only redemption for the sin of consumption.

*The Economist* once said: "Saving is not a virtue in itself – a public good to be encouraged by government, like careful driving or using litter bins. It is an economic decision about the allocation of resources." If everybody's decision was to save half their income, we would all be in a sorry state.

### Prices and sources
Anything that is not consumed is, by definition, saved; and the decision whether to consume or to save is based largely on price. The price of savings in this case is the general level of real interest rates, that is, nominal rates less inflation. Historically these have fluctuated between –4% (in the USA in the 1970s) and 8% (in the USA in the mid-1980s).

Anything too far outside this range is unsustainable. A market with persistently negative real rates is soon going to run out of savers; and one with real rates in double figures is going to be hard-pressed to find profitable homes for the high level of savings that would be attracted to such rates.

Savings come essentially from individuals and from companies. They can, in theory, also come from governments, but it is a rare government these days that is not borrowing from others in order to pay its bills.

In a world of nation states, each state can also attract savings from foreigners. If governments permit (that is, if they remove exchange controls), nations can export or import savings just as easily as they can export or import consumer goods. If left alone, savings will flow across the exchanges from one nation to another in search of the highest rate of return.

**The intermediaries**
There is a host of institutions keen to be the bearer of these savings to those borrowers judged capable of using them productively. These institutions compete with each other, and dangle a different balance of risk and reward with which to entice savings their way.

They fall into a number of categories.

**Short-term financial markets.** These provide the savers and users of funds with a direct interface. They include markets as short-term as the overnight interbank market, in which banks place their surplus funds for the overnight use of other banks with a shortage. They also include markets for instruments like commercial paper (a means for companies to place their surpluses with other companies) and treasury bills (which enable governments to raise funds from individuals and financial institutions). Commercial paper and treasury bills can have a maturity of three months and more.

**Bond markets and stockmarkets.** These are long-term financial markets. Bonds can be issued with a maturity of anything up to 15 years, and shares are issued for eternity. Investors put off by the thought of being locked into financial assets for so long are given reassurance by the existence of secondary markets. These provide liquidity at all times; that is, they enable investors to sell their long-term assets at short-term notice (though maybe at a loss) whenever they wish.

**Banks and other short-term financial institutions.** Basic commercial banks provide savers with a number of different services, from very short-term current accounts to longer-term time deposits. They also provide the core service of money transmission enabling savers to move money from one institution to another without having to carry bundles of notes from door to door.

Traditionally, banks come in a number of

different guises depending on whether their key function is money transmission (commercial banks); the collection of savings (savings banks); the raising of money in financial markets for industry and governments (investment banks); or all of these things (universal banks). In recent years these distinctions have become less and less clear.

**Long-term financial institutions.** These are mainly insurance companies and pension funds, institutions that have become the biggest repositories of developed nations' savings. They collect huge sums of money which they invest mostly in stock and bond markets. In many places tax advantages have greatly enhanced the attractiveness of these institutions as conduits for savings.

Governments and government institutions are not themselves great savers. Nevertheless they do have great influence on the direction in which savings flow for the following reasons.

- Their budget deficits make them large consumers of others' savings.
- National savings schemes' interest rates can be insensitive to market forces. They can thus shift the competitive position of different private-sector financial institutions.
- By the structure of their tax systems, governments almost invariably encourage borrowing at the expense of savings. Not for them the guilt of excessive consumption and inadequate saving.

# DEDICATED FOLLOWERS OF FASHION

How do you tell the difference between a sheep and a banker? Answer 1: the sheep is better dressed. Answer 2: you make a meal of the sheep on Sundays; the banker makes a meal of you every other day of the week.

The greatest similarity between sheep and bankers is their gregariousness. Bankers prefer to work huddled together in the major financial centres of the world. Even when outside those financial centres they huddle together; they are neighbours on the major crossroads of every high street and members of the same clubs.

Their gregariousness would be their own affair if it were confined to geography, but it is not. Bankers are also extremely gregarious in their business activity and this can have dangerous consequences, especially since it is a habit that they seem unable to kick. The history of the industry is spattered with examples ranging from nineteenth-century escapades on Argentine railways to twentieth-century excesses with leveraged buy-outs and ventures into securities' markets.

## Knowing your limits

What bad business habit might their gregariousness be leading them into today? The most likely answer is internationalisation. For behind their current healthy round of cost-cutting (imposed on them by widespread recession) lie ambitions to seize opportunities opened up by various forms of deregulation around the world.

Historically banks have been remarkably parochial, a condition that has often been forced upon them by legislation. It is not long since big Chicago banks like Continental Illinois were allowed only one branch in their home state. All that profligate lending to Latin America in the 1970s was done not out of a global network of offices, but from a single branch in London, with the aid of a sheaf of airline tickets.

## Pan-European moves

At present the internationalisation of financial services is focused on Europe. The single market programme of the European Community and the opening up of eastern Europe have provided extensive new opportunities for cross-border expansion. In the EC the so-called "single passport directive" permits an institution that is authorised to carry out banking business in one member state to do so in all member states.

There is nothing original in all this; European banks have been creeping across each other's borders for years. The Rothschilds, Hambros and Schroders all drifted into London from continental Europe at different times over the past two centuries; and although the British promenade up and down the seafront at Cannes less frequently than they once did, Barclays and Lloyds still have branches there.

## EC momentum

For the most part such moves were motivated by the banks' desire to follow their customers. As the single market has encouraged their customers to cross borders within the Community, so it has encouraged bankers to follow those customers.

One of the biggest moves has been Deutsche Bank's takeover of the UK merchant bank Morgan Grenfell. The deal was surprising for two reasons. First, because it happened in the relatively mature banking markets of northern Europe. Second, because it straddled two very distinct banking cultures: the German universal banking system, where all services are available at one bank; and the UK system, which is split between commercial banking and investment banking.

One of the busiest markets, however, has been in Spain, where a number of cross-border alliances and takeovers followed the defossilisation of the banking system there. Many predict that a similar foreign penetration of the domestic industry will soon occur in Italy, as its banking system too is forced to respond to pressures to liberalise.

## New approaches

There are signs that this new spurt of internationalisation will follow a different pattern from the classic ones of takeover or of building branch networks. For one of the more sober banking discoveries of recent years is the fact that only certain banking services travel well.

Robert Poldermans, a banking guru with Arthur D. Little, has identified certain characteristics that financial products must have if they are to be suitable for selling across borders. They include:

- standard product design;
- susceptibility to central administration; and
- a weak relationship between a customer and his or her existing supplier.

That embraces things like consumer credit. Financial firms already enthusiastically offer consumer loans by direct mail, based on little more than the answers to a standard questionnaire. Thus consumer credit is a standard product, centrally administered. Poldermans's definition likewise covers mortgages.

In general, the link between a customer and the provider of loans is much weaker than that between a customer and the guardian of his or her savings. Whereas consumers will happily take loans from First National Bank of Anywhere, they prefer to deposit their spare cash with Homely Savings Bank. In other words loan products travel better than savings products.

## Co-operative benefits

Foreign banks setting up in new markets have known this for a long time. It has held back what might have been expected to be one of the most natural cross-border alliances in the banking industry, that between the very strong savings bank co-operatives in continental Europe. They have a long tradition of co-operation, yet their savings products are not easily exportable.

The only savings product identified by Mr Poldermans as being likely to travel well was the mutual fund. It is no coincidence that the European Community has issued a special directive to encourage it to do so. Undertakings for collective investments in transferable securities (UCITS) – Eurospeak for mutual funds – can now be marketed anywhere in the Community subject to certain basic safeguards.

## Future disaster

Where in all this might lie the seeds of a future banking disaster? Since banks are not seizing every opportunity to waste large sums of money in opening new branches abroad, or in buying foreign banks, could it be that their enthusiasm for internationalisation is being tempered with the sort of modesty that has been all too lacking in their previous faddish enthusiasms?

That would be easier to believe if it were not for the fact that the selective marketing of particular products (especially loan products) exposes the banks several times over to a danger which has long been dormant. Banks do not know how much any of their services cost them, although they do know that many are sold at a loss in a complicated process of cross-subsidisation. It is conceivable that the latest round of internationalisation could leave them hugely successful at selling hugely loss-making services all over the world.

# INSTITUTIONAL RESPONSIBILITY

There is a group of financial institutions in the West which has developed almost unnoticed into a huge slumbering giant. As yet the giant has not realised its own strength, but times are changing and it may soon bestir itself. Should it then start to flex its muscles in financial markets, it could bring about enormous and unpredictable change.

The slumbering giant is the so-called "long-term financial institutions": insurance companies, pension funds, investment trusts, and so on. Today the assets of US insurance companies alone are worth a staggering $1,500 billion, and the numbers are still growing fast. Upon the investment skills of these institutions hangs the future well-being of millions of people.

Huge sums of money flow into their coffers every day of the year. Although some of this goes into real estate, and some even (as in the case of the British Rail pension fund in the 1970s) into paintings and sculpture, the vast majority of the funds head for the major bond and stockmarkets of the western world. Between them the institutions own significant chunks of all the biggest companies in the USA, Europe and Japan, from IBM to ICI and from Daimler-Benz to Toyota.

## Two types of insurance

Insurance companies sell two types of service. One is straightforward insurance against accidents, called casualty insurance. In return for paying a premium into a pot, a person pools the risk of a particular type of accident with others paying premiums into the same pot. Those among them unfortunate enough to suffer from the accident get compensated out of the pot.

The second type of insurance is called life insurance (or, more correctly, life assurance). It consists of a series of regular payments (like premiums) against a future event that is assured of happening: somebody's death. Upon the death, a lump sum is paid over. As a form of saving it bears similarities to a pension. Companies which run life assurance schemes have to invest wisely in order to meet payment obligations which will not occur until many years later.

Ordinary insurance business does not create this long-term obligation. Most casualty insurance has a fairly short and finite life. The difference between the premiums an insurance company receives from car insurance in a year, and its payouts on car accidents in the year, is its profit, more or less. There is no obligation beyond that.

## Pension power

As long ago as 1979 a former British prime minister, Harold Wilson, was saying that "the growth of pension funds during the 1970s has created the biggest revolution in the British financial scene this century. Surprisingly, it was almost totally unperceived by political or even financial commentators until very recently."

With this growth (which continued even more dramatically in the 1980s) a number of problems have arisen. Perhaps because they grew largely unremarked, pension funds also grew in a haphazard and random way. Unlike the insurance business, there is no body of law dedicated to their structure and regulation. In consequence they have become very private institutions, run by people who want to perpetuate that privacy.

Moreover, the management of pension funds is more nebulous than that of life assurance. It is not concentrated in a few large companies (as insurance is in most countries) and it is not easily measured. Some companies' pension funds have their own independent management, watched over by trustees, some of whom may well be employees of the company; other funds are managed entirely by an outside manager (an investment bank or private management company); and yet others by a mixture of the two.

## Use and abuse

Like other private yet powerful institutions (such as the Freemasons) pension funds arouse suspicion by their devotion to privacy. Occasionally published events encourage those suspicions. In 1976 the UK food company J. Lyons (inventor of the Lyons tea house) was in dire straits; it helped itself to recover by selling some of its properties to its own pension fund. Most of the trustees of the pension fund (including its chairman) were also managers of the company. At the time, such behaviour was not illegal.

Fifteen years later there was no doubt about the illegality of Robert Maxwell's dipping into the pension funds of public companies (of which he was chairman) in order to bolster his own private business empire. After the British publishing tycoon drowned in mysterious circumstances (before any charges could be brought), reputable pension funds rushed to make themselves more accountable to their beneficiaries.

Under certain circumstances it is quite legal for a company to remove assets from its pension fund. This is when it is overfunded, that is, when the fund's assets are more than are needed (actuarially) to meet its obligations to pensioners in the future. In the stockmarket exuberance of the late 1980s many companies found that they were overfunded, and some were quick to use the surplus assets in the fund to top up their own corporate dividend payments. There was little attempt to look at the issue the other way round: could the terms and conditions of the fund's obligations to its pensioners be improved?

The insurance business too has been buffeted by scandal, much of it concentrated on the Lloyd's market in London. This is a centuries-old market for casualty insurance where a few agents were able to syphon off large volumes of premium income into their own pockets; and where the famous "names" – who back the market with all their worldly wealth – were sent reeling by vast unexpected losses that set off a chain of lawsuits.

### Future shock

The long-term institutions should be able to see off these whiffs of scandal in the years to come. But they may continue to be haunted by the prospect of the growing cohorts of the elderly, whose old age will only be made bearable by the institutions' investments in a commercial and industrial base run by shrinking cohorts of the young.

This problem may force them to confront an issue that they have so far largely avoided: their responsibility for the health and prosperity of the industrial companies of which they are increasingly the absentee owner. Occasionally institutions will remove an incompetent managing director and replace him or her with their own choice. But such shows of strength are rare, and more common in the UK than in the USA; there institutional fund managers still prefer to vote with their feet, selling their stock and walking away from any responsibility to change things in "their" company.

# Revolution on the Stock Exchange

The major stockmarkets of the world have probably seen more dramatic changes in the past 20 years than in all their previous existence.

- Technology has had an enormous impact on the way the markets function. It is as if the barrow boys have abandoned their fruit and vegetable stalls, and have instead set up automatic through-the-wall fruit-and-veg dispensers. The days when orders were shouted out across a crowded stock-exchange floor are rapidly disappearing. Stocks and shares are increasingly bought and sold via telephones and computer screens.
- Deregulation has made an enormous difference to the people who trade in stockmarkets. It is as if the fruit market were no longer the exclusive preserve of barrow boys; now it is just an offshoot of a huge supermarket chain. If a barrow boy is sick one day, the supermarket's manager stands in for him.
- Internationalisation has brought about enormous changes in what the barrow boys sell. Stockmarkets were traditionally national; the shares of one country's companies were not generally traded on the stock exchanges of another. However, with the increase in cross-border takeovers and foreign direct investment, and with the development of international groupings like the European Community, stockmarkets too have become international.

Major multinational companies' stocks can now be bought on many different markets around the world. The barrow boys are selling aubergines and rambutan as well as home-grown carrots and potatoes.

## Relative strengths
Pride of place among stockmarkets still goes to

the New York Stock Exchange (NYSE) with its access to the unmatchable pool of US capital. It has begun to become more international, first through the use of American depositary receipts (ADRS) and then through a growing number of foreign companies prepared to go the whole hog and obtain a full listing on the NYSE.

The Tokyo stockmarket has shown the most extraordinary growth in recent years, with its capitalisation increasing more than ten-fold during the 1980s. With this growth it too has become more international, and there are over 120 foreign stocks now listed on the Tokyo stock exchange.

Both the American and Japanese markets have been fuelled largely by their own vast domestic economies. But the stockmarket that has changed most in the past decade (and is perhaps showing the way for others in the future) is the London market, now housed in the International Stock Exchange.

## London's pole position

As the premier international financial centre in Europe, London naturally made a play for pole position in an increasingly unified single European market. It had good reason to hope to win. The language of international finance has long been English, thanks as much to the Americans as to the British; and where the Port of London left off as a roundabout for people, goods and information, Heathrow airport and information technology took over.

The first important step towards making London Europe's premier stockmarket was taken with Big Bang on October 27th 1986. The UK government, worried about the cliquishness of the London Stock Exchange and its inability to compete internationally, set about deregulating it in order to make it more competitive.

Big Bang marked the climax of that process, bringing to an end rules that had restricted who could own a stock-exchange member firm, and also ending the fixed minimum commissions that members had hitherto decided (among themselves) to charge for deals in stocks and shares.

The big City of London banks – with nothing exciting to do since the heavily indebted Mexicans had slunk home with their sombreros low after the international debt crisis of 1982 – saw this as a chance to get into a new business that might provide new opportunities for interesting foreign travel. They rushed to buy the stockbroking firms that all of a sudden became available. A big stake in one of them, Wedd Durlacher Mordaunt, was bought by Barclays Bank for a price which valued the firm at £100m.

Yet the assets of these firms (their staff) could walk out of the door any day. Some of them were tied by contracts (golden handcuffs), but many left as fast as they could find an excuse, shortly to be found earning twice as much in an office just around the corner.

## Automation

In this way a lot of big banks lost a lot of big money. Nevertheless Big Bang did succeed in bringing foreign capital into the London market, and it created a keener awareness of the international potential. Foreign shares were increasingly traded in London, where deregulated prices could easily compete with prices in the shares' domestic markets. The London Stock Exchange changed its name to the International Stock Exchange and began to automate the exchange in order to give it further cost advantages.

Here it scored a big success. SEAQ International (the Stock Exchange Automated Quotation system) took off very quickly when it opened its telephone lines for floorless trading in the late 1980s. By the early 1990s 50 market makers were trading 750 blue-chip company shares from 20 different nations. Market makers merely typed into their computers the number of shares on offer and their proposed price, and the information flashed simultaneously on over 3,000 traders' screens around the world. Deals were then finalised over the telephone.

By the early 1990s the turnover on SEAQ in

Dutch and Swedish shares was already about half the level of the turnover on their domestic markets. For French and Swiss shares it was about 30%. Continental European bourses grew concerned. Paris and Milan prepared their own automated exchanges, while others contemplated how to respond to London's challenge.

## Privatisation

There is one thing, however, that has not changed much on the London market in recent years, and that is the market's major customers. Almost everywhere the number of shares bought by the big long-term financial institutions has increased remorselessly.

That is surprising in view of the widespread popularity of privatisation during the 1980s. In the UK, where £27 billion-worth of state enterprises were sold off during the decade, privatisation came with a crusading zeal. By the time of the sale of the telecommunications giant British Telecom in 1985 a UK government minister was moved to say that the government's aim was now "to build upon our property-owning democracy and to establish a people's capital market". Privatisation was no longer just about raising money for the government, it was about taking capitalism (and share-ownership) to the people.

With the benefit of hindsight, it is clear that it was no such thing. All the evidence suggests that a large number of the people who bought shares in the likes of British Telecom sold them soon after. Others, who bought only a few, hung on to them with the sole intention of leaving them to their grandchildren.

By the end of the 1980s more than 60% of all UK quoted company shares were held by institutions: insurance companies, pension funds, and so on. While there were more individuals owning shares than there had been at the beginning of the decade, those individuals owned a smaller percentage of all the shares available. Somebody has reckoned that the last individual to own a share in the UK will be selling it sometime around the year 2020. It will be a pity if other stockmarkets around the world follow that particular example.

# THE CONVERGENCE OF CORPORATE FINANCE

A nation depends critically upon its ability to provide its manufacturing and service industries with the finance that they need in order to create greater wealth and greater profits. Yet, despite this common purpose, nations have developed very different ways to channel funds to their industry.

Perhaps the most fundamental difference lies in the relative role of banks and stockmarkets. In nations like Germany and Japan, industry's relationship with banks is very close indeed. Germany's biggest manufacturing company, Daimler-Benz, is 28% owned by the biggest bank, Deutsche Bank. Not only does Daimler-Benz (not surprisingly) rely for most of its financial services on Deutsche Bank, but the chairman of its supervisory board is, almost *ex-officio*, the spokesman (that is, the chairman) of Deutsche Bank. If Deutsche Bank does not like what Daimler-Benz is doing it is in a very strong position to stop it.

In Japan almost all big companies have one so-called main bank. The role of the main bank is special; as in Germany, the bank and the company may well be linked by an equity stake, and the company will rely on its main bank for all its short-term financing needs. The main bank will also have access to inside information, and an influence over a client company's management that in many other countries would be seen as unacceptable interference.

## Anglo-Saxon attitudes

In Anglo-Saxon economies industry has a rather different appetite, relying much more on financial markets for money than on financial institutions. Corporate bonds and stocks therefore account for a much higher percentage of Anglo-Saxon companies' external sources of funds.

Relatively heavy dependence on stockmarkets brings demands that can be quite as exacting as those of a German or Japanese bank. Top of the list is the remorseless annual demand for dividends which companies feel unable to resist in case their market capitalisation is cut (and hence their cost of raising new equity increased). Steady annual dividends are paid to supposedly risk-taking Anglo-Saxon investors out of money that could otherwise have been cheap internal funds for financing future investment.

In practice, higher dividend payments do not necessarily mean that Anglo-Saxon companies are at a disadvantage in being forced to depend more on expensive external sources of funds rather than on (cheaper) internal ones. The external/internal ratio is remarkably consistent across cultures.

In Japan this is accounted for by the fact that Japanese corporate profitability is generally lower than it is in the West, which is a consequence of something that common sense tells us must be true: Japanese profit margins are narrower than anybody else's.

## Hostile bids
Another feature that comes with lively stockmarkets is the hostile takeover. In Germany and Japan such a thing is almost unheard of, excluded by closely intertwined relationships between groups of significant shareholders such as founding families and suppliers, as well as banks.

In the UK and the USA hostile takeovers are commonplace, financed by bankers' fickle money and made possible by the vulnerable exposure of a company's ownership to all-comers via a quotation on an open stockmarket.

## Relationships
It is not only the de-institutionalisation of corporate finance that distinguishes Anglo-Saxon economies; it is also the relationships that exist between banks and industry. In the Anglo-Saxon world an industrial company tolerates its bankers; at worst, it is in a constant state of confrontation with them.

The ties that bind the two sides together are not strong. Big US companies use literally hundreds of banks for different bits of business; big Japanese companies will rarely use more than ten. Staff turnover at US and UK banks is also much faster than it is in Japan and Germany. The chief financial officers of US corporations could well find themselves dealing at one of their banks with three different account officers in as many months.

However, this traditional picture has been changing in recent years as a number of different influences have come to bear on financial markets. The most significant of these all end in "ation".

**Internationalisation.** As manufacturers themselves have spread across the globe so have their financiers; sometimes in pursuit of their customers; sometimes in pursuit of the capital that has been increasingly free to move at will around the world's major financial centres. This has brought Japanese banking habits to the north-east of England, for example, and the very first hostile takeover to Japan.

**Deregulation.** The enthusiasm in the 1980s for deregulation had at least two significant effects on corporate finance. First, the freeing up of interest rates in the USA and Japan essentially allowed banks to pay depositors as they wished. That pushed up the price of deposits, and therefore the price of loans, which encouraged companies to seek funds outside the banks.

The granting to all financial institutions of the freedom to offer a much wider range of services meant that there was a much larger number of players in each particular financial market. Company treasurers would be fielding several sales calls a day from bankers who, because they were now empowered to do something, felt that they had to do it.

**Disintermediation.** Partly as a consequence of deregulation, industrial companies found that they were increasingly able to cut banks out of the chain that passes money from an original lender to an ultimate borrower. This process is known as disintermediation, and was strikingly demonstrated by the growth of the commercial paper market in the USA. Commercial paper is a short-term financial instrument issued by corporations. Among the biggest buyers of commercial paper are other corporations.

**Innovation.** Deregulation fostered competition, and nowhere more so than among investment bankers, a community that talks unashamedly of products and marketing. Out of this came one of the most controversial financial products ever created: the junk bond. Strictly speaking this was not a new product but a development of an old one. But it gave a huge section of corporate America access to a corporate bond market; access that had (for some not entirely obvious reason) been previously denied it.

**Securitisation.** The growth of the commercial paper market and of the junk bond market was indicative of yet another "ation": securitisation, the tendency of companies in a number of countries to raise more through the issue of securities of one sort or another, and less by means of loans.

**Privatisation.** Finally, the popularity of privatisation across the capitalist world also changed the face of corporate finance. In the 1980s the UK government alone raised over £25 billion for itself through privatisation. This money increased the stock of private equity capital dramatically.

The net result of all these changes is that corporate finance in the USA, Germany and Japan is becoming more similar, and looks set to continue to converge. It is yet to be seen, however, who will be the main gainer from such convergence.

# Part 2

# A–Z

## ACCEPTANCE

A BILL OF EXCHANGE that has been endorsed by a BANK; that is, a bank has given its GUARANTEE that it will pay the bill should the buyer fail to do so. This is a time-honoured way of financing trade. The exporter whose bill is accepted by a first-class bank can then sell the bill at a DISCOUNT in the financial markets. This improves the exporter's CASH FLOW over what it would have been had it waited for its customer to pay in the normal course of business.

*The Barings Bank crisis of 1890 began when a bond issue of £3.5m for the Buenos Aires Drainage and Waterworks Company failed. The London merchant bank Barings felt obliged to lend to Argentina via acceptance credits instead. Falling raw material prices then frustrated the Argentine government's attempts to repay the credits as they became due. Barings had to be rescued by the Bank of England, but has managed to survive ever since.*

## ACCEPTING HOUSE

A member of an elite band of independent UK merchant banks whose core business was originally that of accepting bills (see ACCEPTANCE). Their reputation was such that any bill they had accepted would, if necessary, be bought by the Bank of England.

In the 1980s all their privileges were extended to a long list of so-called eligible banks, many of them foreign. Since then the houses' once powerful City club – the Accepting Houses Committee (AHC) – has been replaced by the much less significant British Merchant Banks & Securities Houses Association.

## ACCOUNT

There are two meanings.

**1** The balance of a customer's borrowing and lending with a BANK. This type of account can take several forms.

- **Current account.** An account on which cheques can be drawn and an OVERDRAFT arranged. Current accounts do not usually pay significant amounts of INTEREST on positive balances. Charges (although rarely itemised) are usually related to the volume of transactions, the size of the balance on the account and the type of service provided.
- **Deposit account.** An account that is always kept in credit, and on which interest is paid.
- **Savings account.** An account designed specifically to assist customers to accumulate large sums by means of small and regular savings.
- **Budget account.** An account designed to help individuals make bulky bothersome payments (like telephone or electricity bills) more smoothly. Regular payments into the account allow the account-holder to borrow several times the value of each payment. Sometimes such an account is in credit; sometimes it is overdrawn. The plan, however, is that it should have the same balance at the end of a year as it has at the beginning.

**2** An account is the period of two weeks (occasionally three weeks) on the London STOCKMARKET prior to the SETTLEMENT DATE. No payment is required until settlement day for a SECURITY that has been bought within the duration of the preceding account. After deducting holidays, there are 24 accounts within each calendar year.

The free credit period represented by the account gives gamblers a chance to dream about making serious gains without putting any investment up-front. They buy shares right at the beginning of an account, hoping to sell at a PROFIT before the day of reckoning, that is, settlement day.

### ACCRUAL RATE
The rate at which a pension increases each year, usually expressed as a fraction. Most people are

part of a one-eightieth or one-sixtieth pension scheme. This means that for each year that they are in the scheme they receive one-eightieth or one-sixtieth of their pensionable earnings on retirement.

## ACTUAL
The physical COMMODITY or SECURITY underlying a FUTURES contract.

## ACTUARIAL SURPLUS
See OVERFUNDING.

## ACTUARY
Facetiously described as someone who finds accounting too exciting. Actuaries contemplate (then calculate) the probability of death occurring to others within prescribed periods of time. This enables INSURANCE companies and the like to determine what PREMIUM they should charge to those taking out life-assurance policies.

## ADJUSTABLE RATE MORTGAGE
A type of MORTGAGE whose RATE OF INTEREST varies over time, and in line with market rates. Historically, mortgages in the USA have been predominantly fixed-rate. On occasions of great interest-rate turbulence this type of mortgage has got financial institutions into trouble when they have been unable to find suitable liabilities to match their fixed-rate assets.

Institutions which do grant adjustable rate mortgages (ARMS) like to issue long-term bonds to match the rate and MATURITY of the loans they are granting. In the UK the great majority of mortgages are ARMS.

## ADR
See AMERICAN DEPOSITARY RECEIPT.

## ADVANCE/DECLINE RATIO
A measure of the difference between the number of stocks whose price is rising on a market, and the number whose price is falling. In the USA

when this difference itself starts to fall it is believed to indicate that a market has peaked.

**AFLOATS**

Commodities that are on board a ship, shipshape and ready to sail.

**AFTER-HOURS**

Shares that are bought and sold after an official STOCK EXCHANGE has officially closed (usually about 15.30). After-hours trades are treated as having been executed on the following day.

**AGENT**

Someone who acts on behalf of others. For example, an estate agent attempting to sell a property on behalf of the owner, for a fee or for a percentage of the sale price.

The word has a special meaning on the LLOYD's insurance market. It is someone who introduces a member (or NAME) to the market, and advises him or her about it.

**AIBD**

See ASSOCIATION OF INTERNATIONAL BOND DEALERS.

**ALLFINANZ**

An Anglo-German neologism for the increasing coming together of banking and INSURANCE services under one institutional umbrella. Many such institutions have been formed by merger; others by a joint venture between a BANK and an insurance company. Some (like Germany's Deutsche Bank) preferred to go into the new service (in its case insurance) from scratch.

The benefit of Allfinanz is said to come from selling in the same outlet such compatible retail products as consumer loans and life assurance. Yet the two have traditionally been sold in very different ways: the consumer LOAN in a bank BRANCH; life assurance in the customer's own home. Although insurance is increasingly being sold in bank branches, and consumer CREDIT in other ways (for example, by direct mail), changing customers' minds about how they should buy financial products is a slow process.

## ALLOTMENT
The amount of STOCK that is allocated to sub-scribers when an ISSUE of securities is OVERSUB-SCRIBED.

It is also the amount of stock that is given to each member of a SYNDICATE when a new issue is syndicated.

## ALPHA STOCK
The most actively traded shares on the London STOCKMARKET. A category devised by SEAQ, it con-sists of shares in which a continuous TWO-WAY MARKET is guaranteed by market makers. The spe-cific shares that are included in the Alpha group can change from time to time.

## ALTERNATIVE INVESTMENT
A less immediately obvious way of retaining value than securities and BANK deposits; for example, works of art, coins, stamps, jewels or GOLD. Alter-native investments tend to outperform more tradi-tional investments when INFLATION rates are high.

## AMERICAN DEPOSITARY RECEIPT
A certificate issued in the USA in lieu of a foreign SECURITY. The original securities are lodged in a BANK abroad, and the American depositary receipts (ADRS) are traded in the USA to all intents and pur-poses as if they were a domestic STOCK.

An ADR's DIVIDEND is paid in US dollars, so it provides a way for (parochial) American investors to buy foreign securities without hav-ing to go abroad, and without having to switch into foreign currencies.

An increasing number of foreign companies are quoted on US exchanges in their own right. But that is an expensive process, and only an option for those who can cope with the seem-ingly insatiable demand for information of the SECURITIES AND EXCHANGE COMMISSION and other US regulatory bodies.

The traditional market leader in issuing ADRs is Morgan Guaranty Bank, which effectively invented them in 1927. There are now over 120 ADRs quoted on the NEW YORK STOCK EXCHANGE, AMEX and NASDAQ; one-third of them are British.

---

*The American Express salad oil incident is one of financial history's most notorious scams. A client borrowed substantial sums of money against the security of huge tanks of salad oil. When the client disappeared, the tanks turned out to be filled with water, except for a drop or two of oil floating on the top of each one – all that could be seen by the casual observer.*

---

## AMERICAN STOCK EXCHANGE

The USA's second-biggest STOCK EXCHANGE (after the NEW YORK STOCK EXCHANGE). Also based in New York, the American Stock Exchange concentrates on the shares of medium-sized companies that are too small to justify the full expense of a LISTING on the NYSE.

The American Stock Exchange is commonly known as AMEX and less commonly as the Kerb Exchange, a name that was officially dropped in 1953.

## AMEX

See previous entry.

## ANALYST

A person who studies the progress of companies and of industries in order to make judgments and recommendations about the value of different stocks and shares, or about the creditworthiness of different DEBT instruments. Such analysts normally work for financial firms like stockbrokers and INSURANCE companies, for example.

The word analyst is also used to refer to those people who analyse markets from inside manufacturing companies.

---

*The largest attendance at an annual general meeting occurred in April 1961 when 20,100*

---

*shareholders turned up for the AGM of AT&T, the
American Telephone and Telegraph Company.*

## ANNUALISED PERCENTAGE RATE

A standardised measure of the annual RATE OF
INTEREST which enables the rates on different
instruments to be compared. Before the annualised percentage rate (APR) became established as
the yardstick for such comparisons, there were
many alternative ways of expressing interest rates.
Consumers could be easily confused by LOAN
sharks comparing interest-rate "apples" with
interest-rate "pears".

The APR is calculated by the formula:

$$APR = \left[ (1 + \tfrac{x}{100})^y - 1 \right]$$

where x is the rate of interest quoted for a period
of less than a year (for example, 2% a month); and
y is the number of such periods in a year.

## ANNUITY

Originally an investment that bought a fixed
annual payment for the investor (called the annu-
itant) until his or her death. A number of compli-
cations have been added on to that basic format.
For example, the payment of the benefit is nowadays more likely to be quarterly or semi-annual
than annual.

There is also a wide range of specialised annu-
ities.

- **Joint annuity.** The benefit is paid throughout
  the lifetime of two people (usually husband
  and wife) and continues until both are dead.
- **Tontine annuity.** A joint annuity where the
  payment increases as the number of annuitants
  decreases (that is, when the husband dies the
  wife gets a bigger regular payment).
- **Deferred annuity.** The regular payments do
  not begin until after a certain specified period.
- **Perpetual annuity.** The payments go on for
  ever (to survivors that is).

### APPLICATION FORM

Part of the PROSPECTUS for a new ISSUE; that part of it which has to be filled in and returned by those who wish to buy some of the issue. For large new issues, application forms are sometimes published as advertisements in newspapers.

*A British member of Parliament called Keith Best was fined and resigned from Parliament in 1985, after he had been found to have entered six applications for shares in BT, the telecommunications monopoly that the government was selling off. The terms of the issue allowed him to make only one.*

### APR

See ANNUALISED PERCENTAGE RATE.

### ARBITRAGE

The buying and selling of financial instruments on different markets in order to take advantage of price differences between the markets. The markets may be in different countries (the FOREIGN-EXCHANGE markets in London and New York, for instance); or they may just be different markets in the same country.

A typical arbitrage deal might involve buying all the shares of a company quoted on the NEW YORK STOCK EXCHANGE, and reorganising it into three separate bits: one to be sold to a Swiss investor, one to a UK quoted company and one to be floated separately on the AMERICAN STOCK EXCHANGE.

A person who lives by arbitrage is called an arbitrageur.

### ARM

See ADJUSTABLE RATE MORTGAGE.

### ASSET-BACKED SECURITY

A SECURITY that is issued by a financial institution and backed by assets (such as a bunch of mortgages or of car loans) that are on the institution's balance sheet. The assets are placed in trust, and the investor in the security can look to them (and sometimes only to them) for repayment of its INTEREST and PRINCIPAL.

## ASSET COVER

The number of times that a company's DEBT is covered by its NET assets.

## ASSET MANAGEMENT

The art of getting the best return possible from the (financial) assets that an institution owns or manages. This involves finding the ideal balance between the yield from the assets on the one hand, and their RISK, MATURITY and LIQUIDITY on the other.

Financial institutions used to devote much attention to asset management. When there was little competition for savers' deposits, their liabilities took care of themselves. But with the rapid DEREGULATION of financial markets in the 1980s, competition for deposits and savings grew rapidly. With it grew the amount of attention paid to the different game of liabilities management.

## ASSET STRIPPER

A person who buys a company in order to make a PROFIT by peeling off its assets bit by bit, and then selling them. These assets may be separate subsidiaries, or plant and equipment, or property. This process invariably involves the stripping of another sort of asset (the employees) of a number of jobs. This has been largely responsible for giving asset strippers a bad name.

The asset stripper relies on there being a difference in the price of the business as a whole (as valued by a STOCKMARKET, for example) and the sum of the amounts that can be raised for its parts sold separately. Such a possibility arises most commonly when a company is making losses, or a much smaller profit than seems to be justified by its size.

## ASSET VALUE

The market value of all the securities and CASH

held by an INVESTMENT TRUST on a particular day, usually expressed as so much per SHARE.

## ASSOCIATION OF INTERNATIONAL BOND DEALERS

See INTERNATIONAL SECURITIES MARKET ASSOCIATION.

## AT BEST

An order from a customer to a BROKER to buy or sell a certain SECURITY at the best current price available.

## ATM

See following entry.

## AUTOMATED TELLER MACHINE

A machine that can carry out most of the functions of a BANK teller or cashier. Automatic teller machines (ATMS) should be distinguished from CASH dispensers: dispensers only dispense cash; ATMS do much more. They take orders for cheque books, hand out statements and even take in deposits.

Over the last two decades ATMS have been spreading like ivy, through banks' walls and inside their branches. Surprisingly, however, they have not yet (as it was once assumed they would) made large numbers of bank staff redundant.

## AVAL

A sort of continental European ACCEPTANCE; a GUARANTEE stamped on a BILL OF EXCHANGE. It guarantees that a trusted party (such as a BANK) will meet the liability if called upon. The bank usually signs or stamps its name under the words *Pour Aval* or *Bon Pour Aval*.

## AVERAGING

The process of buying more of a certain type of SECURITY as its price falls in order to reduce the average price paid for the security. For example suppose a speculator pays $5 a SHARE for 10,000 shares in First National Bank of Nowhere just before the BANK is linked with massive and criminal laundering of drug money. The bank's share

price plunges to $1. The speculator might then
decide to buy 10,000 more shares at $1 each.

The speculator has thus paid $60,000 for 20,000
shares, averaging the cost per share at $3 and
enabling them to be sold at a PROFIT as soon as the
price of NatBank of Nowhere rises above $3.

**BACK-TO-BACK**

COLLATERAL provided by importers to back CREDIT extended to them by exporters. In the case of importers in developing countries who are buying from developed countries where they are not known, such collateral could be something like a bank DEPOSIT held abroad by the importer.

**BACKWARDATION**

The situation where a COMMODITY due for delivery today fetches a higher price than the same commodity to be delivered at a future date. Backwardation usually occurs where there are temporary log-jams in transport or distribution, which make the commodity temporarily rare.

**BAD DEBT**

A LOAN or a bill that is not paid within a reasonable time of its due-by date, usually because a borrower has gone bankrupt or a customer has CASH-FLOW problems. Bad debts are an inevitable part of business; keeping them under control is an art.

Banks set aside PROVISIONS out of their regular PROFIT to cover the bad debts that they know they will suffer. Without provisions, all of a bad debt has to be taken out of profit in the year in which it occurs.

**BALLOON**

A LOAN whose repayments are not spread evenly over its life. At one stage – towards the loan's MATURITY – the regular dribble of repayments bulges into one or two big balloon repayments that finally wipe the slate clean.

**BANK**

An institution that deals in money and (most significantly) creates money by making loans that do not have to be repaid until some future date. Because of this function, governments have always kept a close eye on their banks.

There are many types of bank (see CENTRAL BANK, CLEARING BANK, CONSORTIUM BANK, INVESTMENT

BANK, MERCHANT BANK, MONEY-CENTER BANK, MUTUAL
SAVINGS BANK, PRIVATE BANK, SAVINGS BANK, UNIVERSAL
BANK) and the main difference between them is
the amount of emphasis that they place on various
fundamental banking services. These include the
following.

**1** Collecting deposits from savers and paying
INTEREST on those deposits (the cost of having the
use of the money over time).
**2** Granting loans to borrowers who seem likely
to make good use of them. This is what banks do
in order to earn enough interest to pay their
depositors.
**3** Money transmission. A service which enables
customers of one bank to transfer funds directly
from their account to the account of somebody
else at another bank. This service is provided by
means of things like a CHEQUE, STANDING ORDER and
DIRECT DEBIT.
**4** Advisory services. In particular, advising companies on how and where to raise new CAPITAL,
and then arranging for the capital to be raised.
**5** Lending their good name to help customers
that they trust. This is fundamental to trade
finance. An exporter gives CREDIT to an importer
because the importer's bank gives its word to the
exporter's bank that payment will be forthcom-
ing. The two banks trust each other; if the
importer and exporter did too they would not
need the banks.
**6** Providing services to other banks in order, for
example, for them to clear funds among themselves. This is a principal function of central
banks.

The first three of these services are fundamental to
the business of commercial banks; the fourth and
fifth are fee-earning services that are at the heart
of the business of merchant banks.

Nowadays banks offer a lot more services such
as INSURANCE, life assurance, and so on (see ALL-
FINANZ).

## BANK FOR INTERNATIONAL SETTLEMENTS

A CENTRAL BANK for central bankers, based in Switzerland. It is a meeting place, a multinational regulatory authority and a CLEARING HOUSE for many nations' RESERVES.

Housed in a round tower near Basel railway station, the Bank for International Settlements (BIS) was set up in 1930 as a private company owned by a number of central banks, one commercial bank (Citibank) and some private individuals.

In the international DEBT crisis of the early 1980s the BIS played a vital role in supplying SHORT-TERM bridging loans that gave dollar-less developing countries time to adjust their economic policies. In the late 1980s it played a less conspicuous role in setting up an international safety net for rapidly deregulating financial markets.

---

*In the 1860s a Munich actress called Spitzeder decided to start a bank, and she promised to pay 20% a year to Bavarian farmers. They handed over 3m gulden before the police realised that Spitzeder was investing it all in herself. She began a long jail sentence in 1872.*

---

## BANKER'S ACCEPTANCE

See ACCEPTANCE.

## BANKER'S DRAFT

An order from a buyer or importer to its BANK instructing it to make a payment to the seller or exporter's bank. The draft is sent to the seller, which presents it to its bank for payment. The seller's bank in turn presents it to the buyer's bank for reimbursement.

## BANKRUPTCY

The condition of a bankrupt, that is, a person who has been adjudged to be unable to pay his or her debts by a court. A bankrupt is deprived of many powers; for example, he or she cannot be a director of a company for a number of years. A bankrupt's property passes into the hands of a TRUSTEE in bankruptcy who is authorised to divide it among the creditors.

*In the last four days of September 1857 150 banks failed in Rhode Island, Maryland, Virginia and Pennsylvania alone.*

## BARGAIN
A deal done at a good price. Also any transaction in stocks and shares on the INTERNATIONAL STOCK EXCHANGE in London.

*The record number of bargains in a single day on the International Stock Exchange was the 114,973 transactions on October 22nd 1987.*

## BARTER
Paying for goods with other goods or services. Barter is at least as old as the Asian silk routes, and often just as devious. It enjoyed a renaissance with the opening up of the former Soviet Union and eastern Europe, regions with a huge demand for imports (particularly of capital goods) but with little foreign currency to pay for them.

Financial institutions are not too keen on barter since it threatens greatly to reduce the need for their services. Some financial institutions, however, have decided that if you cannot beat 'em, join 'em. They have set up specialist barter departments to organise and service the complicated deals that are increasingly being put together.

*The biggest recorded barter deal was of 36m barrels of oil for ten Boeing 747 jets for Royal Saudi Airline in the 1980s.*

## BASIS POINT

A unit of measure used to express small movements in the rate of interest, foreign-exchange rates, or bond yields. One basis point is one-hundredth of one percentage point. Thus the differential between a bond yield of 5.38% and one of 5.79% is 41 basis points.

## BASIS PRICE

See STRIKE PRICE.

## BEAR

An investor who thinks that the price of an individual SECURITY (or of a whole market) is going to fall. A bear, therefore, sells securities in anticipation of being able to rebuy them later at a lower price.

Alternatively, bears will buy FUTURES contracts that commit them to selling securities at a fixed price on a future date. They anticipate that this fixed price will be higher than what they will have to pay for the securities in the spot market on that future date.

A bear market is one that is experiencing a sustained fall in prices. (See also BULL.)

## BEARER SECURITY

A BOND or SHARE certificate that is not registered in the name of its owner. Whoever holds the certificate (or bears it) can collect the INTEREST or DIVIDEND due, usually by detaching a COUPON. A bearer security can be bought or sold without being endorsed; it is as liquid as CASH, and equally vulnerable to theft.

A EUROBOND is a bearer bond. Bearer bonds have the great advantage of being more easily kept out of the tax authorities' eye than normal registered securities.

## BED AND BREAKFASTING

An expression referring to the practice of selling securities on the last day of a tax year and buying them back the next day (the first day of the next tax year). This is done to establish a loss for the first tax year which can then be set off against gains for the purposes of CAPITAL gains tax.

## BELLWETHER
A SECURITY that is seen as a significant indicator of the direction in which a market's prices are moving. For example, IBM's SHARE price is a bellwether for the NEW YORK STOCK EXCHANGE; ICI's share price likewise for the INTERNATIONAL STOCK EXCHANGE. Long-term government bonds of various maturities are usually the bellwethers for national BOND markets.

## BELLS AND WHISTLES
The little extras that are added to basic financial products. For example, the warrants or options that can be attached to simple bonds.

## BENEFICIAL OWNER
The ultimate owner of a SECURITY, that is, the person who receives the benefits associated with the security. The expression is applied in cases where a security is registered in the name of a custodian, someone who holds it in trust for the beneficial owner.

## BERNE UNION
An association of providers of EXPORT CREDIT insurance. Founded in 1934, it has almost 40 members from some 30 countries. It aims to promote "the international acceptance of sound principles of export credit and INSURANCE".

In recent years the association has been primarily concerned with preventing an all-out war among the government agencies that make up the bulk of its membership. Each of them is under continuous political pressure to provide more favourable terms in order to boost their own country's exports.

## BETA
A category of shares created by SEAQ. Beta stock is less actively traded than ALPHA STOCK.

**BETA COEFFICIENT**
See VOLATILITY.

**BID**
The highest price that a prospective buyer is prepared at that moment to pay for something, be it a company, a Van Gogh painting, or a SECURITY.

**BID COSTS**
The costs incurred by a company in bidding for another company. These include the fees of a panoply of advisers such as merchant bankers, lawyers, accountants, and so on. Bid costs have to be borne whether the bid is successful or not.

**BID-OFFER SPREAD**
The difference between the lowest price at which a seller will offer its goods or services, and the highest price that a buyer will bid for them. In the FOREIGN-EXCHANGE market, for example, banks' exchange rate quotations give two prices: the highest price that the BANK (as a buyer) will offer for a particular currency; and the lowest price it will accept for that currency (as a seller).

**BIG BANG**
What occurs on the day when a significant financial market removes a swathe of old-fashioned rules and regulations. The most famous Big Bang occurred at the London Stock Exchange (renamed the INTERNATIONAL STOCK EXCHANGE) on October 27th 1986. From that date:

- stockbrokers were obliged to abandon their long-standing fixed scale of COMMISSION;
- for the first time foreigners were allowed to own a majority stake in a UK BROKER; and
- DUAL CAPACITY was introduced, allowing brokers to be market makers and vice-versa.

The biggest bang on the day, however, came from the STOCK EXCHANGE's newly computerised dealing and quotations system which collapsed under the strain.

The US equivalent was called Mayday and took place on May 1st 1975, the day on which minimum commissions were abolished on the NEW YORK STOCK EXCHANGE.

## BILL OF EXCHANGE

A written instruction to a buyer (importer) to pay a seller (exporter) a defined amount of money before a certain date. In the UK a CHEQUE is a bill of exchange, still governed in important respects by the Bills of Exchange Act of 1882.

## BILL OF LADING

The set of documents giving title to goods while they are in transit. On the documents is a brief description of the goods and where they are going. The bill of lading is signed by the shipper, which undertakes to deliver the goods in the same condition as it receives them.

## BIS

See BANK FOR INTERNATIONAL SETTLEMENTS.

## BLACK MONDAY

STOCKMARKET history is riddled with black days. Black Monday was October 19th 1987, when virtually all the world's stockmarkets tumbled by all-time record amounts.

Black Tuesday was October 29th 1929, the blackest day of the Great Crash; others talk of Black Thursday, October 24th 1929, the day when the markets first began to fall heavily.

The UK has its own Black Wednesday, September 9th 1992, the day when FOREIGN-EXCHANGE market speculators forced the pound to abandon the EXCHANGE RATE MECHANISM.

## BLOCK TRADING

Trading in big blocks of shares. On the NEW YORK STOCK EXCHANGE any deal of more than 10,000 shares, or $1m-worth of bonds, is a block trade. Such deals are usually carried out by financial institutions, and certain stockbrokers specialise in block trading.

The daily number of block trades is recorded and watched closely by market analysts. It gives an indication of how active financial institutions are vis-à-vis individuals.

## BLUE CHIP
The STOCK of a first-rate industrial company, which is one with a long record of continuous and steadily rising PROFIT, and of uninterrupted DIVIDEND payments.

## BLUE-SKY LAWS
Legislation passed by individual states in the USA regulating the sale of corporate securities in that state. The legislation is designed to protect investors from FRAUD.

*Charles Blunt, brother of John Blunt, the leading fraudster in the South Sea Bubble, cut his throat in September 1720, the month the bubble burst. Contemporary press reports said he had committed suicide "upon some discontent".*

## BOND
An INTEREST-bearing instrument issued by governments, corporations and some other organisations, and sold to investors in order to raise CAPITAL. Bonds may be bought and sold many times over in the SECONDARY MARKET before they are finally redeemed. They are sold at a DISCOUNT (or PREMIUM) to their face value, such discount (or premium) reflecting the difference between the (fixed) interest rate on the bond's COUPON and the current market interest rate. (See also BEARER SECURITY and JUNK BOND.)

## BONUS ISSUE
See SCRIP ISSUE.

## BOOK
The accounting record of a business, or of financial securities. Book-keeping is the maintaining of

the ledgers and other books of record of a business, or of an ISSUE of securities. With every securities issue and SYNDICATED LOAN, one BANK (or brokerage firm) is selected to manage the book (for a fee). Today most book-keeping is done using computers.

## BOOK RUNNER
The BANK or securities firm that is responsible for the documentation and general management following the ISSUE of a SECURITY or a SYNDICATED LOAN.

## BOOK VALUE
The value of a company's assets as expressed in its balance sheet. This can be less than the assets' market value since accounting convention may dictate that the assets be included in the accounts at their purchase price. INFLATION alone may well have ensured that this is less than the assets' current market value.

## BOUGHT LEDGER
The department in a company that deals with its payments. It puts into effect the company's policy on CREDIT: how much to grant to its creditors, and over what period of time.

## BOURSE
The continental European expression for STOCK EXCHANGE.

## BRANCH
The retail outlet of a BANK; the shops around the country where it collects deposits, makes loans and arranges money-transmission services. In Chicago, where banks are allowed few branches, they can be as big as major railway stations; in other places they can be little more than a hole in a wall. (See also SATELLITE BANKING.)

## BRIDGING LOAN
A LOAN that spans the short period from now to the time when a more long-term credit FACILITY can be arranged for whatever payment has to be made.

Bridging loans are commonly used for house purchase (before a long-term MORTGAGE has been properly set up), and for financially distressed developing countries (see BANK FOR INTERNATIONAL SETTLEMENTS).

## BROKER

An individual or a firm that buys and sells financial instruments on behalf of others. A broker is an AGENT who works for investors and financial institutions. His or her reward comes in the form of COMMISSION based on the value of the transactions that the broker undertakes. This gives the broker system an in-built incentive to CHURN clients' portfolios.

*In 1927 Juan Leguia, son of the president of Peru, was paid $450,000 by J & W Seligman and an affiliate of the National City Bank for his services in connection with a $50m loan, which the two firms marketed, to Peru. The loan eventually went into default, and President Leguia was violently removed from office.*

## BUCKET SHOP

In modern parlance a bucket shop is a place where cheap airline tickets are bought. Before 1930 it referred to a BROKER who took orders to buy securities but did not execute them. He hung on to his client's money in the belief that the client would be sure to predict price movements wrongly. The broker planned to buy the shares later for the client at a cheaper price and pocket the difference.

When the client predicted the price movements correctly the broker often decided to emigrate. Such practices were made illegal in the USA in 1930, and the expression "bucket shop" dropped out of use.

## BUDGET

A plan (or estimate) of revenue and expenditure for a specific period in the future. In a balanced budget revenue and expenditure are equal.

Budgets are necessary because income and expenditure do not occur at the same time. In large companies budgeting is an annual process, with future income and expenditure broken down into monthly (or even weekly) estimates.

A budget may take several months to prepare. It starts with an estimate of sales and income, then moves on to estimate the expenditure on materials, administration, production, research, distribution, and so on, that will be needed for that level of sales.

National budgeting is the process of doing this for a whole nation.

CAPITAL budgets are made up for periods in excess of one year. They make estimates of future capital expenditure, and of the borrowing required for it.

### BUDGET ACCOUNT
See ACCOUNT.

### BUILDING SOCIETY
A type of financial institution that grew up in the industrial towns of the UK in the nineteenth century (and from which to a large extent they took their names, such as Bradford, Burnley, Halifax, Leeds, Leicester). Building societies were designed initially to do little more than take in local short-term savings and put them out as long-term loans for house-purchase (mortgages). In recent years, however, they have been allowed to become much more competitive with banks. The banks have encroached on to their traditional MORTGAGE territory, and the societies have begun to offer money-transmission services and loans for purposes other than house purchase.

### BULL
A person who expects the price of a SECURITY (or of a whole securities market) to rise. The opposite of a BEAR. Bulls will buy shares now expecting to be able to sell them later at a higher price. Bulls

who are losing their nerve are known as stale bulls.

## BULLDOG BOND
A bond denominated in sterling but issued by a non-British borrower.

## BULLET
A LOAN on which all the PRINCIPAL is repaid in one go at the end of the period of the loan. During the life of the loan the borrower pays INTEREST only.

## BUNDESBANK
Germany's CENTRAL BANK, housed in a modern block in a Frankfurt suburb since it had to leave its Berlin headquarters after the second world war. As central banks go, the Bundesbank is unusually independent of government, and is the zealous guardian of Germany's low-INFLATION economy. However, its purely national constitution has brought it into conflict with the increasingly pan-European responsibilities of the German government.

## BUNNY BOND
A BOND where the investor has the option to receive INTEREST in CASH or in the form of more of the same bond.

## BUY-BACK
An agreement in a sales CONTRACT whereby the vendor agrees to buy back the property if certain conditions are (or are not) met within a certain period. For example, an agreement to buy back a house if the purchaser has to move on within a certain period of time; or an agreement to buy back a stake in a company if it fails to reach a pre-agreed level of PROFIT during its first year in new hands.

## BUYER CREDIT
A medium- to long-term LOAN granted to a foreign buyer of exported goods. The loan is given by the exporter's BANK and usually carries the GUARANTEE

of the exporter's national EXPORT CREDIT agency.

The CONSENSUS agreement decrees that buyer credits should not exceed a certain (high) percentage of the price of the goods being bought. The buyer therefore has to find at least some of the purchase price itself.

## BUYER'S MARKET

A market in which there is a plentiful supply of commodities (or securities or whatever), and in which (as a consequence) prices are weak.

## CALL

A demand made by a company on a shareholder for payment for shares that have been issued as PARTLY PAID.

## CALL OPTION

A CONTRACT to buy a certain number of shares at a stated price (the STRIKE PRICE) within a specified period of time. A call option will be exercised when the SPOT PRICE goes above the strike price. If it is not exercised, the option expires at the end of the specified period of time.

## CAMEL

An acronym for the five things that BANK supervisors look for most keenly when examining a bank.

1 CAPITAL adequacy.
2 Asset quality.
3 Management quality.
4 Earnings.
5 LIQUIDITY.

## CAP

A ceiling imposed on the amount of INTEREST and/or CAPITAL that is to be repaid on a LOAN. It is particularly applicable to the US ADJUSTABLE RATE MORTGAGE where there can be:

- annual adjustment caps which place a restriction on the amount of interest that can be paid in one year;
- a life-of-loan cap which places a ceiling on the amount of interest that can be paid on the loan throughout its life;
- a payment cap, which limits the amount of change in the monthly repayments from year to year.

## CAPITAL

The money used to run a business. Capital is raised by issuing shares and long-term DEBT instruments. The balance of a company's ordinary shares, preference shares and long-term debt constitutes its capital structure. Together with its retained PROFIT, these make up the company's capital employed. The key relationship between debt and EQUITY is known as GEARING (or leverage in the USA).

For financial institutions capital is particularly important; it is a safety net against sudden losses arising from BAD DEBT, bad management, or skulduggery. When a CENTRAL BANK wants to find out whether a commercial BANK has adequate capital it looks closely at the institution's so-called free capital: its paid-up capital, bonds and RESERVES, less the amount it has tied up in fixed assets.

## CAPITAL ALLOWANCE
Part of the amount paid for capital equipment that can be set against income for the purposes of calculating a company's taxable PROFIT. The demand for capital equipment in an economy can thus be controlled to some extent by governments' fine-tuning of these allowances, both by their amount and by the things that they can be set against. For example, allowances might vary as to the period over which the capital expenditure can be set off (20% a year for five years) or by the percentage that can be set off (60% in year one, but no more).

## CAPITAL EMPLOYED
The CAPITAL in use in a business. There is no universally agreed definition of what this includes, but it is usually taken to mean NET assets (that is, current assets plus fixed assets less current liabilities) plus bank loans and overdrafts.

## CAPITAL FLIGHT
See FLIGHT CAPITAL.

## CAPITAL GAIN
The PROFIT from the sale of a CAPITAL asset (such as a BOND or SHARE). In most countries capital gains are subject to special tax rules. In a few countries, however, capital gains are treated in the same way as income for taxation purposes.

**CAPITAL MARKET**

Any market in the long-term financial instruments (like shares and bonds) that make up a company's CAPITAL.

**CAPITAL RATIO**

The ratio of a BANK'S CAPITAL and RESERVES to its total assets. In many countries this is not allowed to exceed a prescribed ceiling.

**CAPITALISATION**

The value of a company based on the price of its shares on a STOCKMARKET (that is, the price per SHARE times the number of shares in ISSUE).

More generally, capitalisation is the attribution of a capital value to a stream of income. It is the amount that would have to be invested now in order to produce a particular income stream in the future.

**CARRY BACK OR CARRY FORWARD**

The capacity to shift tax advantages, or pension payment privileges, from one year into another, either back into a fiscal year that has ended, or forward into one that has not yet begun.

**CASH**

Ready money; most obviously notes and coin, but also liquid assets that can be turned into ready money rapidly and without loss. The demand for cash varies throughout the year, being particularly strong, for example, in Christian countries at Christmas time.

---

*In 1907 a US bank was so desperate for cash that it bought the cash receipts from the Harvard-Yale football match. It paid $48 in interest for every $1,000 it took.*

---

**CASH FLOW**

The amount of money flowing through an organisation (or, indeed, an individual) in a given period. For a company, cash flow is the sum of its new borrowings plus money from any SHARE issues, plus its trading PROFIT, plus any DEPRECIA-TION. A company can be recording rising profits year-by-year while its CASH is ebbing, not flowing. Laker Airways, the failed British airline, was a prime example. It reported increasing profits every year at the end of the 1970s. But all its size-able cash flow was going into paying for new investments (that is aircraft). There was nothing left to repay its rising debts.

## CASH MARKET
See SPOT PRICE.

## CASH ON DELIVERY
Commonly known by its acronym COD, cash on delivery means goods or services must be paid for in full at the time they are handed over to the buyer. The American term is collect on delivery.

## CATS
See CERTIFICATE OF ACCRUAL ON TREASURY SECURITIES.

## CBOE
See CHICAGO BOARD OF OPTIONS EXCHANGE.

## CBOT
See CHICAGO BOARD OF TRADE.

## CD
See CERTIFICATE OF DEPOSIT.

## CEDEL
See CENTRALE DE LIVRAISON DE VALEURS MOBILIERES.

## CENTRAL BANK
The institution that is at the hub of a nation's mon-etary and financial system. Each major developed country has one (see BUNDESBANK and FEDERAL RESERVE SYSTEM), but they do not all do the same things.

All central banks carry out some combination of five different functions.

1 They act as banker to the government.
2 They act as banker to commercial banks.
3 They supervise the banking system.
4 They print and issue the nation's currency.
5 They are the LENDER OF LAST RESORT, a back-stop that can print money in a severe financial crisis.

**CENTRALE DE LIVRAISON DE VALEURS MOBILIÈRES**
A computerised CLEARING HOUSE for Eurobonds and other international securities. Based in Luxembourg, Centrale de Livraison de Valeurs Mobilières (CEDEL) was founded in 1971, and is owned by a large number of financial institutions. Its only real competitor is Euroclear, which began in 1968 and is based in Brussels.

**CERTIFICATE OF ACCRUAL ON TREASURY SECURITIES**
An American financial invention. Certificates of accrual on treasury securities (CATS) are US Treasury bonds that pay no INTEREST during their life (see ZERO-COUPON BOND). They are therefore sold at a deep DISCOUNT to their face value, and redeemed at their full face value on MATURITY.

CATS also stands for Computer Assisted Trading System, a piece of software developed by the Toronto Stock Exchange, now used widely around the globe.

**CERTIFICATE OF DEPOSIT**
A certificate issued by a bank to indicate ownership of a large DEPOSIT (usually over $10,000). A certificate of deposit (CD) is a NEGOTIABLE INSTRUMENT and can be bought and sold on a SECONDARY MARKET between the time that it is issued and the time that it is redeemed.

**CFTC**
See COMMODITIES FUTURES TRADING COMMISSION.

**CHARGE**
There are at least two meanings.

1 Property pledged or taken as SECURITY for a LOAN, as in "the BUILDING SOCIETY that lent them the

money to buy their own home has a charge on the house".

**2** The cost of goods or services, particularly of financial services; for example, BANK charges, the fees paid to banks by their customers for services. The basis for these charges is often opaque, and bank customers have only recently begun to demand clear statements of how the charges are calculated.

## CHARGE CARD

A plastic card that allows its owner to buy goods before paying for them. Charge cards are usually issued by department stores to their regular customers. The customers can then spend as much as they like in the store until the day each month when they have to pay the outstanding charges in full.

Some charge cards have a credit facility attached which allows the repayment to be spread over time. There is a fine distinction between a charge card and a TRAVEL AND ENTERTAINMENT CARD.

## CHARTISM

The art of predicting future price movements of STOCK and other securities by looking at past price movements. Thus chartists spend their time examining charts which plot price movements over time. They look for recurring patterns (like a head and two shoulders), and on the basis of these patterns they forecast future price movements. (See HEAD AND SHOULDERS.)

The popularity of chartism tends to be cyclical.

---

*In 1931 Albert Wiggin, chairman of the Chase Bank in New York and a man earning some $250,000 a year, continued to sell Peruvian and Chilean bonds at their old prices after having received information that the Chilean and Peruvian governments had stopped paying interest on the bonds. This was one of many frauds committed by Mr Wiggin.*

---

## CHEQUE

A BILL OF EXCHANGE drawn on a BANK, and payable on demand. With the development of plastic cards and the growth of the AUTOMATED TELLER MACHINE, the demise of the cheque has long been predicted. But announcements of its death have been premature. In 1976 68% of all non-cash transactions in the UK were made by cheque; by 1992 the figure had only fallen to 50%.

- A cheque is stopped when a bank refuses to clear it, that is, refuses to transfer the funds as requested (frequently because the funds are not there). The bank sends the cheque back to the BRANCH it came from.
- A post-dated cheque is one which has a future date on it, before which it cannot be cleared.
- A crossed cheque can only be credited to a payee's bank account; it cannot be paid in CASH.
- A blank cheque is one where the amount to be paid is left blank, to be filled in by the payee.

(See also TRAVELLER'S CHEQUE and EUROCHEQUE.)

## CHEQUE CLEARING

A has an ACCOUNT at Bank X and B has an account at Bank Y. When A writes a CHEQUE to B it passes between Bank X and Y; they clear it by debiting A's account and crediting B's. Cheque clearing began in the coffee houses of London's Lombard Street where bank clerks would meet in order to exchange bundles of cheques among themselves.

## CHICAGO BOARD OF OPTIONS EXCHANGE

The largest options market in the USA, and a subsidiary of the CHICAGO BOARD OF TRADE. The Chicago Board of Options Exchange (CBOE) was founded in 1973.

## CHICAGO BOARD OF TRADE

The largest FUTURES exchange in the world. The Chicago Board of Trade (CBOT) and the CHICAGO

MERCANTILE EXCHANGE between them handle about half of all the world's trading in futures. The CBOT is stronger in financial futures; the CME in commodities.

## CHICAGO MERCANTILE EXCHANGE
Set up in 1919, the Chicago Mercantile Exchange (CME) is a major CASH market and FUTURES market for the trading of commodities. It pioneered trading in livestock futures (pork bellies, and so on).

## CHINESE WALL
A partition between two parts of a financial institution that are supposed to act independently of each other. Their independence is required in order to avoid conflicts of interest. For example, a divide between the corporate finance side of an INVESTMENT BANK (involved in new SHARE issues) and its FUND MANAGEMENT side. Without separation, the fund managers might be tempted to buy the corporate financiers' new issues in order to help the bank out of difficulty, rather than because they were a good investment for the fund.

Chinese walls need not be physical; but many institutions do put different parts of their business (between which conflicts might arise) in different buildings.

## CHURN
To trade excessively in the shares of a client's account, with the result that the BROKER makes a large amount of COMMISSION income (based on turnover). In the USA churning is illegal, if it can be proved that the SHARE sales were largely inappropriate for the client.

## CIRCULAR TRANSACTION
When two companies carry out reciprocal transactions in order to inflate each other's accounts artificially. For example, A sells B $1m of goods, and B immediately sells A $1m of the same goods. After the transaction nothing has changed except for the stated turnover of each company, which is $1m higher than it would otherwise have been.

## The City

The name of the part of London that is roughly bounded by St Paul's Cathedral to the west and the Tower of London to the east. It is also the collective name of the many financial institutions in the area, as in "the City thinks that the RATE OF INTEREST is set to fall". People who work in the City are either "City gents" or "City slickers".

The City (also known as the Square Mile, which gives an approximate idea of its size) is home to most foreign banks in the world's busiest international financial centre. They are there because traditionally they had to be within easy walking distance of their supervisor, the Bank of England, which sits pretty well in the centre of the City.

Over the years the City has seen off challenges from many rival foreign financial centres, and even from different parts of London (such as the giant modern development at Canary Wharf).

## City banks

The dozen large commercial banks that dominate the Japanese financial system (banks like Sumitomo and Dai-Ichi Kangyo). They not only lend vast amounts to Japanese industry (and not very much to Japanese consumers), but they are also intertwined in the large industrial/financial complexes (called *zaibatsu*) which many believe account for much of Japan's post-war economic success. City banks are not only very close to their industrial customers, they are also able to wield great influence over them.

## Class action

A lawsuit brought about by individuals in their position as members of a class. For example, a legal action (alleging fraud, say) initiated by an individual shareholder on behalf of all shareholders.

## Clearing bank

A type of commercial BANK in the UK which has the authority to clear cheques (see CHEQUE CLEAR-

ING). In practice, a clearing bank is today little different from a UNIVERSAL BANK.

## CLEARING HOUSE

A firm or agency that handles the paperwork involved in transferring money or a SECURITY from one owner to another. A clearing house enables those institutions that use it to net off their credits and debits against each other at the end of each working day. They then need make only one payment transfer to each other per day. This simplifies their paperwork considerably.

## CLOSED-END FUND

A fund which has a fixed number of shares. Investors who want to buy into the fund have to buy its shares in a SECONDARY MARKET. A closed-end fund is the opposite of an open-end fund (like a MUTUAL FUND) which simply issues new units every time a new investor wants to join.

In the UK a closed-end fund is called an INVESTMENT TRUST.

## CLOSING PRICE

The official STOCK-EXCHANGE price of a SHARE at the end of the exchange's trading day.

## CME

See CHICAGO MERCANTILE EXCHANGE.

## CMO

See COLLATERALISED MORTGAGE OBLIGATION.

## COB

See COMMISSION DES OPERATIONS DE BOURSE.

## COD

See CASH ON DELIVERY.

## CO-FINANCING

A technique for bringing the international muscle of institutions such as the WORLD BANK and the Asian Development Bank together with the financial clout of commercial banks. Projects in developing countries are co-financed jointly by the international institution and a group of commercial banks.

Co-financing gives the banks the comfort of knowing that borrowers rarely if ever default on loans from the World Bank *et al*. The World Bank benefits from the extra billions that commercial banks can bring to a negotiating table.

## COLLATERAL
Property that is provided by a third party as SECURITY for a borrower, as in "my father let me use his house as collateral for a LOAN". The fine distinction between collateral (which is provided by a third party) and security (which is provided by the borrower) still exists in the UK. In the USA the two words are virtually indistinguishable.

## COLLATERALISED MORTGAGE OBLIGATION
A SECURITY that is backed by a bunch of MORTGAGE bonds; that is, the issuer of a collateralised mortgage obligation (CMO) has the CMO as a liability and mortgage bonds as an asset. The PRINCIPAL and INTEREST payments on the mortgage bonds pay the holder of the CMO. This is part of the circuitous route sometimes followed by money on its way from a saver to somebody who wants to buy a house.

## COMEX
See COMMODITY EXCHANGE INC.

## COMFORT LETTER
A letter required by US securities legislation. It is written by an independent auditor and guarantees that the information appearing in a PROSPECTUS has not altered materially in the time between the preparation of the prospectus and its distribution to the public.

## COMMERCIAL PAPER
Short-term DEBT instruments issued by top-notch companies and banks. Born first in the US finan-

cial markets, commercial paper spread rapidly throughout Europe and the Far East during the 1980s. By 1992 commercial paper worth over $500 billion was outstanding in the USA.

Commercial paper has a maturity of 5–365 days (most frequently 30–90), and is issued in dollops that can be as small as $10,000 or as large as $1m. It is sold at a DISCOUNT to its face value, and is rarely INTEREST-bearing. When issued in the EUROMARKET, such instruments are known as Eurocommercial paper.

## COMMERZBANK INDEX
The main INDEX of the German STOCK EXCHANGE. The exchange has been based in Frankfurt since the second world war, and was in Berlin before it.

## COMMISSION
The reward of an AGENT, usually expressed as a percentage of the sales that the agent generates on behalf of his or her client. In most industries there are accepted standard percentage commissions for different types of business. Any negotiation of commissions is done around these base points.

## COMMISSION DES OPERATIONS DE BOURSE
The official watchdog of the Paris BOURSE. The Commission des Opérations de Bourse (COB) is a government agency that supervises new listings on the bourse, monitors takeovers and looks out for INSIDER DEALING. The COB's power and influence grew in line with the rapid growth of the French STOCKMARKET in the 1980s.

## COMMITMENT FEE
A payment made to a lender in return for the GUARANTEE of a LOAN (up to a certain size) as and when needed. The fee is usually a fraction of 1% of the amount committed.

## COMMITTEE ON UNIFORM SECURITIES IDENTIFICATION PROCEDURES
Commonly known by its acronym CUSIP, the Committee on Uniform Securities Identification Proce-

dures is an organisation that assigns numbers to securities that uniquely identify them. Each ISSUE has its own nine-digit number printed on the face of every document.

## COMMODITY

Goods that are usually sold in bulk, and often on the floor of an exchange. Common commodities are grains, metals and certain foodstuffs (like pork bellies, orange juice and coffee). The most valuable commodities of all (by turnover) are oil and GOLD.

## COMMODITY EXCHANGE INC.

A US commodities market founded in 1870. The Commodity Exchange Inc. (Comex) now trades in FUTURES and options as well as its traditional spot markets in metals such as GOLD, silver, copper and aluminium. Together with the London Metal Exchange, it dominates world trading in metals.

## COMMODITIES FUTURES TRADING COMMISSION

The Commodities Futures Trading Commission (CFTC) was set up in 1979 by the US Congress to regulate US commodity FUTURES markets.

## COMMUTATION

The exchange of part of a future pension for CASH now.

## COMPENSATING BALANCE

An amount that a customer is asked to deposit with a BANK when the bank makes a LOAN to the customer. On the surface this sounds rather odd. Why borrow money from a bank simply in order to put it back into the bank?

The rationale for compensating balances lies in a time when there were strict limits on the RATE OF INTEREST that could be charged to lenders. Banks that wanted to charge more would charge the top legal rate and then insist that borrowers also deposit a certain amount (interest-free) with the bank. This free balance would compensate for the interest payments that the bank was unable to collect on the loan.

## COMPENSATION FUND
A fund run by the INTERNATIONAL STOCK EXCHANGE to compensate investors who are owed money by a member firm that has gone bust.

## COMPLIANCE OFFICER
An employee of a securities firm who is appointed to make sure that the firm follows the (increasingly complex) rules laid down by financial-market regulators.

## CONCERT PARTY
A group of investors who act together (and in secret) to try to gain control of a company. Each buys a small stake which, when combined, gives them control.

## CONFLICT OF INTEREST
An occasion where the interests of a person or firm in one guise are in conflict with the interests of the person or firm in another guise. For example, a bank advising a company in its battle against a takeover will have a conflict of interest if it is also a shareholder in the bidding company. CHINESE WALLS are designed to prevent conflicts of interest.

## CONSENSUS
The common name for the International Agreement for Guidelines on Officially Supported Export Credit. The consensus is an agreement between member countries of the OECD on how far they will go in subsidising the RATE OF INTEREST on loans to buyers of their country's exports. The minimum interest rates that they agree to permit vary according to whether the importing country is relatively rich, intermediate, or relatively poor.

## CONSORTIUM BANK
A BANK owned by a group of other banks from a number of different countries. Consortium banks were popular in the 1970s when they were seen

as a way to gain a toehold in the markets represented by all the other banks in the consortium.

Many of these consortium arrangements have been disbanded because the idea outgrew its usefulness. Banks eventually became confident enough to go into new markets on their own.

## CONSUMER CREDIT

A LOAN granted to someone to enable him or her to buy consumer goods like cars, washing machines, and so on. In many countries there are specific laws about consumer credit, designed to prevent the consumer from being exploited by ruthless loan sharks. In the USA at least 12 different government agencies are concerned in some way with ensuring that consumer credit is granted fairly.

## CONTANGO

The RATE OF INTEREST charged to a buyer of a SECURITY on the INTERNATIONAL STOCK EXCHANGE who wants to carry a transaction over from one ACCOUNT to another.

Contango also denotes the situation where prices for future delivery of commodities are higher than for present delivery. This is the opposite of BACKWARDATION and is sometimes known as forwardation.

## CONTRACT

In general, a legally binding agreement between two parties that one will supply goods or services to the other for a specified price.

A contract is also the unit in which options are traded, normally representing an OPTION on 1,000 shares of an underlying SECURITY.

In FUTURES, a contract is an agreement to buy or sell specific amounts of a COMMODITY in the future.

## CONVERTIBLE

The capacity of one FINANCIAL INSTRUMENT to be converted into another. The expression is usually applied to bonds or preference shares that can be converted into ordinary shares at a specified time, and at the request of the bondholder.

## COOKE COMMITTEE

A committee formed within the BANK FOR INTERNA-
TIONAL SETTLEMENTS. Under the chairmanship of an
official of the Bank of England, Peter Cooke, it
was set up to work out ways in which different
countries could harmonise their rules on the
amount of CAPITAL that banks should be forced to
keep. The committee's recommendations were
published in 1988 and have been acted upon in
most developed countries.

## CORRESPONDENT BANK

Before banks opened their own branches across
the globe they used to manage their international
business by setting up a network of loose relationships with other banks in different countries.
These so-called correspondent banks provided
services in their home market for the others in the
network, and vice versa.

## COST OF CAPITAL

An average of the costs of a company's various
types of CAPITAL: ordinary shares, preference
shares, debentures, bonds, loans, retained PROFIT,
and so on. The cost of a LOAN is the INTEREST paid
on it; the cost of a SHARE is the DIVIDEND. The tax
treatment of these costs (interest and dividends)
varies in such a way that it is usually more attractive for companies to borrow than to raise new
EQUITY.

## COUPON

A piece of paper attached to a BEARER SECURITY giving the bearer the right to the income (INTEREST or
DIVIDEND) that comes with the security. To collect
income due, the bearer must detach the coupon
and present it to the paying AGENT of the issuer of
the security.

Coupon is also used to refer to the interest rate
itself.

## COVER

Funds to provide protection against loss (as in
INSURANCE cover), or to guarantee payment of a

liability (as in DIVIDEND cover). Dividend cover refers to the number of times that a company's dividend payment can be covered by its total post-tax PROFIT (earnings).

---

*On October 29th 1929, Black Tuesday, 16.4m shares were traded on the New York Stock Exchange, a record that remained unbroken until 1968.*

---

## CRASH

What happens when a STOCKMARKET falls unnaturally, and a lot of financial institutions go bust at the same time. The greatest crash this century occurred in 1929 in the USA. Since then crashes have been much smaller, or the figment of a writer's imagination.

J.K. Galbraith, in his classic book *The Great Crash 1929*, attributed that particular crash to five main causes.

**1** The poor distribution of income in American society. The top 5% of the population was reckoned to be receiving 33% of all personal income.
**2** Bad corporate structure. The 1920s was a decade of stockmarket fraudsters and crooks who bled corporations of huge sums of money.
**3** Bad banking structure. There were too many independent units, and the structure was such that the failure of one of them led to others collapsing in a domino effect.
**4** The USA's foreign balance. There was a declining trade surplus for the first time in modern history.
**5** The poor state of economic intelligence at the time. The government made decisions that were contrary to the best interests of the economy, but there was inadequate data on what actually was the state of the economy.

---

*Between September 3rd 1929 and July 2nd 1932 the Dow Jones Industrial Average index of the New York stockmarket fell from 381.7 to 41.2, its lowest figure ever, wiping out over $70 billion.*

---

## CREDIT

A LOAN, or the ability to raise a loan, as in "he bought the washing machine on credit" and "her credit at the bank is good".

## CREDIT CARD

A rectangular piece of plastic that empowers its owner to buy goods and services, and to buy them on CREDIT. The use of credit cards has grown rapidly in recent years, from 450m transactions in the UK in 1986 to over 700m in 1992.

Most credit cards are issued by banks, but some are provided by retailers. The credit card business is dominated by two powerful brand names, Visa and Mastercard. These are marketing organisations to which the banks that issue cards are affiliated. (See also CHARGE CARD.)

## CREDIT LINE

A CREDIT limit agreed between a customer and a BANK, which the customer can draw down as and when required.

## CREDIT NOTE

A written message informing a customer that his or her account with a supplier has been credited (and by how much). Credit notes are frequently used when a customer returns goods as being below standard, or when there has been a short shipment.

## CREDIT RATING

A formal assessment of a company's creditworthiness, and of its capacity to meet payment schedules on time. A credit rating is often obtained by a trader dealing with a new customer for the first time. It may come from the client's bankers or existing suppliers, or from one of the specialist agencies (like Dun & Bradstreet) that provide such ratings, for a fee.

## CREDIT UNION

An organisation in which a group of people with a common bond get together to pool their savings. They then lend those savings to each other. Credit unions are popular in the USA where they are non-PROFIT-making organisations with total assets of over $100 billion.

*After the fall of the Austrian bank Creditanstalt in Vienna in May 1931, there was a run on German banks by investor/speculators who did not know the difference between Austria and Germany.*
Charles Kindleberger, *Manias, Panics and Crashes*

### CUM DIV

The opposite of EX-DIV: a SHARE being sold together with the right to a DIVIDEND that has been declared but not yet paid. Similarly, cum rights is a share that is being sold with the right to take up a new offer of shares.

### CURRENT ACCOUNT

See ACCOUNT.

### CURRENT RATIO

The ratio of a business's current liabilities to its current assets.

- Current assets = CASH, bank deposits and other items that can be quickly turned into cash.
- Current liabilities = SHORT-TERM loans and trade CREDIT.
- Current assets minus current liabilities = WORKING CAPITAL. (See also CAPITAL EMPLOYED.)

The current ratio is used as a guide to a company's solvency. It has only limited use in comparing companies across industries, however. The appropriate current ratio for a company depends on the industrial sector that it belongs to, and on the normal terms of trade in that industry. These terms can vary greatly.

### CUSHION BOND

A BOND that can be retired early, that is, it can be

called in before it reaches MATURITY. There is a stated price (the CALL price) at which such bonds can be called, and this inevitably holds down the SECONDARY-MARKET price of cushion bonds. However, it also helps to stabilise the price of the bonds in times of turbulent INTEREST rates.

## CUSIP

See COMMITTEE ON UNIFORM SECURITIES IDENTIFICATION PROCEDURES.

## CUSTODIAN

Somebody (usually a BANK or a lawyer) who holds an investor's securities on behalf of the investor. A custodian handles everything that arises from ownership of the securities, such as the collection of income, voting at meetings, exercising rights, and so on.

## DAWN RAID

The purchase of a large chunk of EQUITY in a quoted company early one morning before the STOCKMARKET has opened, often by simultaneous buying over the telephone. Brokers get prior commitments to sell from investors; and the whole deal is wrapped up before the market can catch a whiff of takeover, and be tempted to push up the company's SHARE price.

Famous dawn raids in the 1980s included the purchase by Allianz, a giant German INSURANCE company (from a country that feigns to disapprove of such takeover tactics), of 29.9% of Eagle Star, a UK insurance company. Allianz failed to consummate the takeover, but it soon sold on its stake in Eagle Star to B.A.T, a diversified conglomerate, for a PROFIT of £166m.

## DEBENTURE

A long-term DEBT instrument, often secured on the general creditworthiness of the issuer rather than on any specific asset. When a company is being liquidated, debenture holders have a right to the company's leftovers before ordinary bondholders.

## DEBIT CARD

A piece of plastic much like a CREDIT CARD, except that it gives the holder no CREDIT. A debit card is passed through an electronic reading device at a point of sale. It thus debits the holder's bank ACCOUNT automatically (and immediately) with the value of the sale.

## DEBT

An obligation of one person to pay something (usually money) to another.

## DEBT SERVICE RATIO

The ratio of a country's annual repayments on its foreign DEBT to the value of its annual HARD-CURRENCY export earnings. Bankers use the ratio as a (first-stab) guide to a country's creditworthiness.

For many Latin American countries in the 1980s the ratio was well over 100%. All their hard-currency export earnings (and more) went to service their debt to foreign banks and governments.

## DEFAULT

Failure to repay a LOAN according to the terms of a CONTRACT. Once a borrower is in default there are several legal moves that a lender can make to try and recover the money, or to get hold of any underlying SECURITY backing the loan.

---

*You can't cheat an honest man.*
W.C. Fields

---

## DEFEASANCE

The placing of assets, like CASH and treasury bills, in trust by a BOND issuer. All the INTEREST and PRINCIPAL due on the bond is subsequently repaid out of these assets, by the TRUSTEE.

## DELIVERY

The transfer of title in a FINANCIAL INSTRUMENT from one owner to another. Hence delivery date, delivery month, and so on, the time when delivery is to be made.

In COMMODITY markets there are three classes of delivery.

- **Current delivery.** Delivery in the current calendar month.
- **Nearby delivery.** Delivery in the next calendar month.
- **Distant delivery.** Delivery in a month that is further away.

## DEPOSIT

There are several meanings.

**1** Money left as SECURITY before receipt of a service, such as a tenant might give a landlord before moving into a furnished property, or a telephone company might demand before connecting a line for a new customer.
**2** Natural resources found underground, as in

"South Africa's rich mineral deposits".

**3** Money left with a BANK for safe-keeping. Such deposits come in many different forms.

- **Demand deposit.** Money that can be withdrawn from a bank on demand or without notice. Also known as sight deposits, and usually non-INTEREST-bearing.
- **Savings deposit.** A sort of piggy bank ACCOUNT, designed for regular savings that are rarely withdrawn. It pays interest, but at below market rates.
- **Time deposit.** A deposit that can be withdrawn from a bank only after a specified period of time; for example, a three-month deposit, or a six-month deposit. These deposits pay interest at close-to-market rates, and are also known as fixed deposits.

### DEPOSIT PROTECTION

An INSURANCE scheme into which banks pay a PREMIUM in order to protect depositors against loss should the BANK go bust. Such schemes usually give limited protection, covering small deposits up to a certain amount (£10,000 in the UK) and insuring larger deposits only up to that amount. This tempts big depositors to spread their money around a number of institutions to get the maximum insurance COVER.

The main argument against these schemes is that they give badly run institutions a competitive advantage, because small depositors become indifferent to the institution that they leave their money with. (See FEDERAL DEPOSIT INSURANCE CORPORATION.)

### DEPRECIATION

The effect of the passage of time (wear and tear or technical obsolescence, for example) on the value of assets; recognition that the value of an asset at one end of an accounting year is different from its value at the other end. Accountants deduct an amount from annual PROFIT to take account of depreciation. (In calculating real CASH FLOW this amount has to be added back.)

Accountants use three main ways of calculating depreciation for the purposes of a company's books.

- **The straight-line method.** This takes an estimated scrap value of the asset at the end of its life, and subtracts this from its original cost. This is then divided by the number of years of useful life that the asset is expected to have.
- **The reducing balance method.** This takes a fixed percentage of the value of the asset last year and sets that aside out of PROFIT; and so on, every year.
- **The inflation-adjusted method.** This tries to take account of the fact (ignored by other methods) that the cost of replacing an asset at the end of its life will usually be greater (if only because of INFLATION) than the original cost of the asset. It sets aside, out of profit each year, an amount adjusted for the rate of inflation during the year.

All these methods ignore the fact that in a fast-changing technological world most assets are unlikely to be replaced with anything like themselves. In some cases (with computer networks, for example) the cost of replacement may be considerably less than the original cost, inflation notwithstanding.

---

*Roger Babson did badly in the 1929 depression by being right too soon. He got his clients out of the market in 1928.*
Charles Kindleberger, *Manias, Panics and Crashes*

---

## DEREGULATION

The process of removing legal or quasi-legal restrictions on the types of business done, or on the prices charged, within a particular industry. The aim of most deregulation is to increase competition by increasing the freedom of players in the industry.

In the 1980s many industries (including airlines, telecoms, banking and stockbroking) were deregulated in a number of developed countries. In the USA the removal of INTEREST-rate ceilings (called Regulation Q) was one example of price deregulation; in the UK the introduction of DUAL CAPACITY in the STOCKMARKET was an example of non-price deregulation.

Regulation has not always arisen as a whim of despotic governments. It is often there to protect consumers. For example, if airlines are allowed to compete too fiercely safety standards may fall, with fatal consequences. Likewise, if banks compete too fiercely their deposits may be put at risk, and savers may lose their money.

## DERIVATIVES

General term for financial assets that are "derived" from other financial assets – for example, an option to buy a treasury bond: the option (one financial asset) is derived from the bond (the other financial asset). Regulators worry that markets for derivatives treacherously undermine markets for the original underlying assets.

## DEVALUATION

A sudden downward jerk in the value of a currency vis-a-vis other currencies. Devaluations occur when a country's costs have risen faster than those of its competitors, and when its exports are no longer competitive in price.

Devaluations are exacerbated by the activity of speculators in the FOREIGN-EXCHANGE markets. They buy and sell vast quantities of currencies in anticipation of a devaluation.

Devaluations can result in huge relative changes in a currency's value; 10% overnight, for example. This can wipe out any ordinary exporter's PROFIT at a stroke, which is one good reason why exporters prefer to work within a framework of relatively fixed exchange rates.

---

*Dictum Meum Pactum (My word is my bond)*
Motto of the International Stock Exchange

---

## DIFFERENCE

The balance due to the client of a London STOCK-BROKER who has both bought and sold securities during an ACCOUNT.

## DILUTION

When a company issues more shares, and sells them for less than their market price, the value of each existing SHARE is diluted. The total value of the company is being divided into a larger number of little pieces (that is shares). Hence the value that attaches to each little piece gets smaller.

Companies sometimes talk about their fully diluted EARNINGS PER SHARE. This refers to the earnings per share when all shares are included: ordinary shares plus any convertible securities (that is, convertible into shares), and all warrants and STOCK options.

## DIRECT DEBIT

An instruction from a BANK's customer asking the bank regularly to debit his or her ACCOUNT with the amount demanded by a named creditor. Direct debits are designed to make it easy to pay regular but varying bills (like those of utilities). For many years they were resisted by bank customers, who were nervous of the way they took control of their finances out of their hands.

## DISCOUNT

There are two meanings.

**1** The verb means to sell at a reduced price.
**2** The noun refers to the reduction in price itself. A CASH discount is a reduction in price given to someone who pays immediately for goods, in cash or in a cash equivalent. A trade discount is a reduction in price given to someone who is in the same trade as the vendor. For example, by a wholesaler of garments to the owner of a fashion boutique.

When a bill is sold at a discount to its face value, the discount represents the INTEREST forgone between the time of the sale and the date that the bill matures.

## DISCOUNT HOUSE
See DISCOUNT WINDOW.

## DISCOUNT RATE
In general, a RATE OF INTEREST paid by the sale of a FINANCIAL INSTRUMENT for less than the PRINCIPAL repayment due on MATURITY. In particular, the interest rate at which a CENTRAL BANK discounts government bonds and other first-class DEBT instruments to commercial banks; or the rate at which central banks lend to commercial banks, using the bills as COLLATERAL.

## DISCOUNT WINDOW
A facility provided by central banks whereby commercial banks can lodge their surplus RESERVES with the CENTRAL BANK, or top up their reserves against the SECURITY of their top-quality assets. Until recently, this function was carried out in the UK by a small number of separate institutions called Discount Houses.

## DISCRETIONARY ACCOUNT
An ACCOUNT that an investor has with a BROKER, and which gives the broker discretion to act on behalf of the investor without consultation. This discretion may only apply within certain pre-agreed limits.

## DISINTERMEDIATION
The exclusion of financial intermediaries (like banks) from the process of allocating savings. This can happen in several ways.

- A company may choose to raise EQUITY, or issue bonds, directly in the financial markets rather than borrow from its BANK.
- A government may choose to raise revenue by issuing attractive savings bonds that are sold directly to the public, rather than by the more traditional way of selling treasury bonds to banks.

To some extent disintermediation is a function of the economic cycle. Market rates tend to move ahead of bank INTEREST rates. So when rates are rising, investors prefer to put their money directly into the markets, and borrowers are happy to pay marginally more for easy access to this money. When rates are falling, bank rates lag behind market rates. Investors then switch their money out of the markets, and into financial institutions.

In the longer term, with the creation of a wider variety of more sophisticated financial market instruments, the opportunities for disintermediation will increase.

## DIVIDEND

That part of the earnings of a company that is distributed to its shareholders. Payment of a dividend is not automatic. It is decided upon by the company, and declared by its board of directors. In the USA this usually takes place every three months; in most other countries it occurs every six months.

Dividends on preference shares are paid at a fixed rate; but on all other shares (in theory) they vary. Many companies, however, find that the RISK from cutting their dividend from one year to the next is considerable. Their SHARE price might fall, and the cost of raising new CAPITAL rise in consequence.

Hence companies go to great lengths to maintain (and if possible increase) their dividends year on year. This has at least two important consequences.

- CASH FLOW for other purposes (such as further capital investment) is often squeezed in order to pay dividends. Some companies go so far as to increase their bank borrowing in order to maintain their dividend.
- Shareholders (supposedly RISK-taking investors) become like the holders of treasury bonds, secure in their expectation of a steady future income (see GILTS).

## DIVIDEND COVER

The number of times that a company's annual dividends can be divided into its annual earnings. Thus if a company's after-tax earnings in a year are $20m, and it pays out $2.5m in dividends that year, its dividend cover is eight.

This is similar to the dividend payout ratio, a concept popular in the USA. The dividend payout ratio is the percentage of the company's earnings paid to shareholders in CASH. With old mature industries this tends to be high (and the dividend cover, therefore, low). But for young growing businesses that need CAPITAL for reinvestment, it tends to be low (and the dividend cover high).

## DOCUMENTARY CREDIT

A method of financing trade. Banks provide the buyer of goods with credit to pay the exporter on the strength of documents which prove that the buyer has proper title to the goods. This is useful when documents reach the buyer more quickly than the goods themselves.

In the mid-1980s more than half of all documentary credits lodged with banks by UK companies were rejected. They were either too late in arriving, or they were incorrectly completed.

## DOUBLE-TAXATION AGREEMENT

It is a fundamental principle of tax law in most nations that the same income should not be taxed twice. In consequence, there is a network of agreements between pairs of nations that seek to avoid taxing income in one country when it has already been taxed in another.

This applies in particular to income that arises in one country, but which is remitted to a resident in another. Double taxation can also occur when income passes from one taxable entity (like a corporation) to another (like a shareholder). Attempts to reduce the double taxation of dividends (paid out of a company's taxed income to taxable individuals) have been less widespread than the attempts to eliminate the taxation of the same income in two fiscal jurisdictions.

## DOW JONES INDEXES

Dow Jones, the company which publishes the WALL STREET JOURNAL, also gives its name to the most famous STOCKMARKET index in the world. The Dow Jones Industrial average (instituted in October 1896) is a closely watched INDEX based on the average prices of a selection of about 30 companies quoted on the NEW YORK STOCK EXCHANGE. It gives an indication of the rate and direction in which the stockmarket as a whole is moving.

There are other less widely reported Dow Jones indexes. They include an index of public utility SHARE prices, and an index of railway company share prices.

*The record fall in the Dow Jones Industrial average on a single day was 508 points (22.6%) on October 19th 1987 (Black Monday). The record rise was 186.8 points, two days later.*

## DOWNGRADE

A reduction in the RATING of a company, or of its DEBT securities.

## DRAWDOWN

Making use of funds that have been made available under a bank FACILITY.

## DROP-LOCK SECURITY

A short-term FLOATING-RATE NOTE or BOND that has a trigger rate, that is, a rate at which it automatically converts into either another FRN or a longer-term fixed-rate bond.

## DUAL CAPACITY

The ability of the same financial institution to be both STOCKBROKER (that is AGENT) and stock JOBBER or MARKET MAKER (that is principal). (See also BIG BANG.) In any business being an agent and a principal inevitably leads to a potential CONFLICT OF INTEREST. In stockbroking, for example, it presents opportunities to put good deals (retrospectively) on the institution's own books, while placing loss-making deals on the books of clients.

### Due date
The date when an INTEREST or PRINCIPAL payment becomes due.

### Due diligence
The thorough search of a business done either by the potential manager of a new ISSUE of the company's securities; or by a company intending to take over the business.

The purpose of due diligence (normally carried out by accountants or financial experts) is to check that the company's sales and general performance are as it claims they are. In the case of a possible takeover this is a delicate exercise. The company carrying out the due diligence has made no binding commitment to buy the business that it is examining. Should it back out of the negotiations it may have obtained commercially sensitive information for nothing. On the other hand, only rarely can a vendor hope to sell a business without giving the purchaser some chance to look at the books in advance of a sale.

## EARNINGS PER SHARE

A measure of the total return earned by a company on its ORDINARY SHARE capital: the NET profit of the company divided by the number of ordinary shares in issue. Net PROFIT is the gross profit (receipts minus costs) less DEPRECIATION, INTEREST charges, PREFERENCE SHARE payments and tax.

A company that makes a profit of $10m and has 2m shares outstanding has earnings per share (EPS) of $5. EPS is seen as a particularly helpful guide to a company's past, present and future performance. (See also DILUTION.)

## EBRD

See EUROPEAN BANK FOR RECONSTRUCTION AND DEVELOPMENT.

## ECU

See EUROPEAN CURRENCY UNIT.

## EFTPOS

See ELECTRONIC FUNDS TRANSFER AT THE POINT OF SALE

## EGIBI

Possibly the first recorded BANK in history. Mr Egibi, the bank's founder, lived in Damascus in the latter part of the reign of the Babylonian king Sennacherib (705–681BC). A stone tablet recording the bank's first loan is in the British Museum.

## EIB

See EUROPEAN INVESTMENT BANK.

## ELECTRONIC FUNDS TRANSFER AT THE POINT OF SALE

A way of paying for shopping electronically, commonly known by its acronym EFTPOS. A plastic card gives the retailer electronic access to a customer's bank ACCOUNT. The account is debited immediately and automatically with the cost of the goods. (See also DEBIT CARD.)

The disadvantage of electronic payment systems from the customer's point of view is that they are immediate. There are none of those helpful 3–4 day delays between the time an old-fashioned CHEQUE is handed over and the time it is debited from the payer's account. With EFTPOS, moreover, any mistakes have to be rectified after payment has been made, which can be a difficult job for customers.

### EMPLOYEE STOCK OWNERSHIP PLAN

An American scheme designed to encourage employees to buy STOCK in the companies they work for. There are tax advantages to such schemes; companies can deduct for tax purposes any dividends paid to employees under an employee stock ownership plan (ESOP).

### EMS

See EUROPEAN MONETARY SYSTEM.

### ENDORSEMENT

The signature on the back of a CHEQUE (or similar FINANCIAL INSTRUMENT) which transfers ownership of the instrument from the signatory to the bearer. A bearer instrument, such as an open cheque, does not need endorsement.

### ENDOWMENT MORTGAGE

A MORTGAGE linked with a life-assurance policy. During the life of the mortgage, the mortgagee only pays INTEREST on it. However, he or she also pays premiums on a policy which matures at the same time as the end of the loan. The capital sum assured by the policy covers the PRINCIPAL that has to be repaid on the mortgage.

### EPS

See EARNINGS PER SHARE.

### EQUITY

The ownership interest of shareholders in a company, as in "he launched a new company last year, and he has 20% of the equity". On the company's balance sheet, equity is what is left over when all the company's external liabilities have been deducted from its assets.

Equity has also come to mean the excess or surplus value of a capital asset over and above the

DEBT still owed on the asset. For example, the amount by which the market value of the securities in a customer's MARGIN ACCOUNT with a BROKER exceed the debt still due on the account; or the amount by which the market value of a house exceeds the MORTGAGE on the house.

---

*Robert Schuyler, president of the New York & New Haven railroad (and of many other companies besides), absconded to Europe in 1854 with almost $2m in cash from fraudulently selling stock in the railroad.*

---

## ERM
See EXCHANGE RATE MECHANISM.

### ESCROW ACCOUNT
A bank ACCOUNT kept by a third party on behalf of two others who are (usually) in dispute about its rightful ownership. The disputing parties try to set out conditions under which they will agree to let the money be released. When these conditions are met, the third party releases the funds.

A notorious recent escrow account was the one set up to hold Iran's deposits with western banks after the shah's downfall, and before it could be decided where the deposits rightfully belonged.

## ESOP
See EMPLOYEE STOCK OWNERSHIP PLAN.

---

*The highest tax demand in history was for $336m on the estate of Howard Hughes.*

---

## EUROBOND
A BOND issued by a company or a government, with two peculiar characteristics.

- It is issued in a market other than that of its currency of denomination.
- The banks that issue it sell it internationally, not just in one domestic market. ρτ$

---

Thus, if Germany's Deutsche Bank were to issue a dollar bond for the UK's ICI, and to sell it around the world, it would be a Eurobond. If it were to sell the bond only in Germany it would be a foreign bond. Eurobonds are peculiar in having no home base whose government can support them should their market collapse.

## EUROCHEQUE

A payment system developed by European banks. It enables travellers around Europe to cash cheques up to a certain maximum value when backed by a standardised Eurocheque GUARANTEE card.

## EUROCLEAR

See CEDEL.

## EUROMARKET

A market in financial instruments that are held in countries other than that which issued the currency in which they are denominated: for example, the market for dollar deposits in Europe (that is Eurodollars), or the market for Deutschmarks (Eurodeutschmarks) in the USA. Dollars held in the Far East are more commonly referred to as Asiadollars than Eurodollars.

Legend has it that the first Eurodollar was created by a Russian communist eager to own dollars, but not eager to keep them in the USA. The Russian decided to keep them in Europe instead, and a lot of other people soon thought it was a good idea too. The Euromarket today is worth a few thousand billion dollars.

## EUROPEAN BANK FOR RECONSTRUCTION AND DEVELOPMENT

A special institution set up to channel aid to eastern Europe. Although created largely on the initiative of the European Community, the European Bank for Reconstruction and Development (EBRD) has 40 member countries. It opened its doors for business (in London) in 1991 with plans to grant 40% of its loans to the public sectors of eastern

Europe, and 60% to the growing private sectors.

## EUROPEAN CURRENCY UNIT
The most likely name of a single European currency, if there is ever such a thing. The European currency unit (ecu) is an artificial currency based on a basket of European currencies. It has been gradually expanding its uses since it was first created by the European Community at the end of 1978. Its purpose then was to act as a reserve asset and as a means of settlement in the EUROPEAN MONETARY SYSTEM. Now it appears in many guises.

- Deposits and loans (particularly mortgages) denominated in ecus are offered by a number of banks.
- Many of the European Commission's payments to subcontractors are denominated in ecus.
- The ecu is actively traded in the FOREIGN-EXCHANGE market.
- There is a substantial ecu BOND market.
- The EUROPEAN INVESTMENT BANK denominates its accounts in ecus.

The composition of the ecu is subject to review every five years. From September 1989 it was made up of the following percentages of the various member states' national currencies.

| | |
|---|---|
| Deutschmark | 30.10 |
| French franc | 19.00 |
| UK pound | 13.00 |
| Italian lira | 10.15 |
| Dutch guilder | 9.40 |
| Belgian franc | 7.60 |
| Spanish peseta | 5.30 |
| Danish krone | 2.45 |
| Irish punt | 1.10 |
| Greek drachma | 0.80 |
| Portuguese escudo | 0.80 |
| Luxembourg franc | 0.30 |

(See also SPECIAL DRAWING RIGHTS.)

## EUROPEAN INVESTMENT BANK

A BANK created in 1957 by the Treaty of Rome (the treaty which first established the existence of the European Community). The European Investment Bank (EIB) acts as a development bank for Europe, using its good name to borrow cheaply on international capital markets, and then lending these (cheap) funds to borrowers in the EC and associate member states.

Most EIB loans are for terms of 7–12 years. The bank has certain priorities. It favours lending for the following.

- Depressed EC areas like Portugal, Ireland and much of Spain.
- The development of European technology.
- Infrastructure projects that involve more than one member country of the EC, like the Channel Tunnel.
- Projects that further a particular interest of the Community.

## EUROPEAN MONETARY SYSTEM

A scheme to manage the way in which European currencies' exchange rates move against each other. The European Monetary System (EMS) started on March 13th 1979 as the successor of the snake, the first concerted attempt to dampen wilder fluctuations in exchange rates since the dollar had been allowed to float freely in 1971.

There are three mechanisms at the heart of the EMS.

- The EXCHANGE RATE MECHANISM.
- Accounting and settlement mechanisms in which central banks swap some of their RESERVES for ecus (a mere accounting device). They then carry out transactions among themselves in these ecus. (See EUROPEAN CURRENCY UNIT.)
- CREDIT mechanisms which enable central banks to obtain loans from other member states' central banks when (and if) they need to bolster up their currency, in order to keep it within the limits of the ERM, for example.

The controversial Maastricht Treaty, signed by the EC member states, plans to take the EMS several giant steps further on. It provides a schedule to implement European monetary union through a system of permanently interlocked exchange rates and a single monetary policy. It is designed to lead to the adoption of a single currency, possibly by the early years of the next century.

## EXCHANGE CONTROL

The method by which governments attempt to control the flow of currency in and out of a country; both foreign currencies and the government's own currency. The UK maintained strict exchange controls for a number of years after the second world war. It only abolished them in 1979. France abolished its controls even later.

## EXCHANGE RATE MECHANISM

A central part of the EUROPEAN MONETARY SYSTEM. The Exchange Rate Mechanism (ERM) is an agreement to maintain exchange rates among member states of the European Community within agreed limits, thus guaranteeing a degree of monetary stability within the boundaries of the EC.

## EX-DIV

An indication given next to a quoted SHARE price showing that the price does not include payment of a DIVIDEND that has been declared by the company but not paid. Ex-div means that the dividend is to be paid to the previous owner of the share.

Likewise, ex-rights means that a share price does not include a recent RIGHTS ISSUE. The rights may either remain with the previous owner, or be sold separately. Ex-new is similar to ex-rights: the purchaser is not buying a right to new shares. (See also CUM DIV.)

## EXERCISE

Making use of a right that is available in a CONTRACT; for example, exercising an OPTION to purchase a SHARE at a certain price within a certain time.

It can also refer to the conversion of a convertible SECURITY into a share.

## EXERCISE PRICE
See STRIKE PRICE.

## EXPIRY DATE
The last day on which a particular right (to buy shares at an advantageous price, for example) can be exercised.

## EXPORT CREDIT
A LOAN to an exporter to tide it over the period between the time when its goods are sent abroad, and the time when it receives payment for them. With exports of large capital goods that time can be anything up to several years.

## EXTERNAL FUNDS
Sources of funds that are available to a company from outside the company itself. Thus the proceeds of a BOND issue or a bank LOAN are external funds; retained PROFIT is an internal source of funds (see INTERNAL FUNDS).

## FACILITY

A banking service (such as an OVERDRAFT facility) that is made available to customers for their use as and when they please. A facility letter is a letter from a bank to whomsoever it may concern confirming in writing the details of a specific LOAN that has been made available to a customer.

## FACTORING

The business of collecting someone else's debts on their behalf. A company sells its receivables (that is, invoices unpaid by its creditors) to a factor (often the subsidiary of a BANK) at a DISCOUNT. The factor then sets out to collect the money owed. Its PROFIT comes once it has collected more than the discounted price it paid for the debts.

The company that sells its debts to a factor gets a helpful boost to its CASH FLOW.

Factoring can include any or all of the following.

- Maintaining the company's sales ledger.
- Managing the company's CREDIT control; that is, making sure that it does not give customers excessively long periods to repay.
- The actual collection of unpaid DEBT.
- INSURANCE cover against BAD DEBT.

Factoring is divided into disclosed and undisclosed. Disclosed factoring, in which the factor lets the debtors know that it is collecting payments on behalf of the client, is increasingly common. Undisclosed factoring (also known as confidential invoice discounting) allows the client to conceal the fact that it has employed a factor, which is sometimes seen as the corporate equivalent of a rat catcher.

## FANNIE MAE

See FEDERAL NATIONAL MORTGAGE ASSOCIATION.

---

*A London banker called Henry Fauntleroy forged notes in order to keep his bank afloat. He was executed for his crime in 1824.*

---

## FDIC
See FEDERAL DEPOSIT INSURANCE CORPORATION.

### FED FUNDS RATE
The rate at which US banks lend their surplus RESERVES to each other overnight. The reserves are generally non-INTEREST bearing deposits held with the FEDERAL RESERVE SYSTEM, and banks hold them in order to meet their required CAPITAL RATIO.

Since it is set afresh every day by the market, the fed funds rate is taken as a particularly sensitive indicator of the way in which US interest rates in general are moving.

### FEDERAL DEPOSIT INSURANCE CORPORATION
The USA's DEPOSIT PROTECTION fund, established in 1933 in the depths of the Great Depression. The Federal Deposit Insurance Corporation (FDIC) recently changed its name to the Bank Insurance Fund (BIF), and now insures all deposits up to $100,000 at banks that take out INSURANCE cover with it.

A similar institution does a similar job for the USA's troubled savings and loan associations. Formerly called the Federal Savings and Loan Insurance Corporation (FSLIC), it too recently changed its name to the Savings Association Insurance Fund (SAIF).

### FEDERAL HOME LOAN MORTGAGE CORPORATION
Commonly known as Freddie Mac, a semi-public US body which guarantees mortgages and finances them by issuing securities. It is largely owned by savings banks, and is similar to the FEDERAL NATIONAL MORTGAGE ASSOCIATION.

### FEDERAL NATIONAL MORTGAGE ASSOCIATION
Commonly known as Fannie Mae, a company created by the US Congress to support the secondary MORTGAGE market. It buys and sells mortgages, and is financed by the issue of bonds. At times it has owned as many as 10% of all US mortgages. Its shares are quoted on the NEW YORK STOCK EXCHANGE.

## FEDERAL RESERVE SYSTEM

Commonly known as the Fed, the CENTRAL BANK of the USA and thus the guardian of the value of the dollar. The Fed is both the regulator of banks in the USA and the controller of the money supply. It works through 12 regional federal reserve banks spread across the country. Each is owned by banks in its area, and each has nine directors serving a three-year term of office.

At the pinnacle of the system is the Federal Reserve Board, comprising seven governors based in Washington, DC. Each of them is appointed by the US president for a 14-year term, which is a long time for people who are rarely young when they start the job.

The Fed carries out the usual monetary and FOREIGN-EXCHANGE responsibilities of a central bank. In addition, it is the supervisor of US bank holding companies. In practice, it keeps an eye on all US banks, for whom it is the lender of last resort.

## FIDUCIARY DEPOSIT

This is a Swiss speciality. A BANK takes a DEPOSIT and lends it on to someone else, entirely at the depositor's own RISK. One of the big benefits of this for the bank is that the deposit remains off its balance sheet (so it does not have to set aside expensive RESERVES against it), yet the bank still makes a return on the transaction. The advantage for the depositor is a higher RATE OF INTEREST and the veil of Swiss secrecy.

Most fiduciary deposits are simply passed on to other banks to become straightforward Eurocurrency deposits.

## FIMBRA

See FINANCIAL INTERMEDIARIES MANAGERS AND BROKERS REGULATORY ASSOCIATION.

## FINANCE HOUSE

A UK institution that began by specialising in HIRE PURCHASE. Most of the big ones have become subsidiaries of major commercial banks, and have been busily expanding their range of services.

## FINANCIAL CENTRE

Any place in which, for historical or fiscal reasons, more than an average amount of financial business is transacted. Centres can range from the big and indisputable (like London) to the small and ambitious (like Jersey or the Cayman Islands).

## FINANCIAL INSTRUMENT

Documentary evidence of the ownership of a financial asset; for example, BILL OF EXCHANGE, CERTIFICATE OF DEPOSIT, government BOND, SHARE, STOCK, and so on.

## FINANCIAL INTERMEDIARIES MANAGERS AND BROKERS REGULATORY ASSOCIATION

A self-regulatory body in the City of London set up as part of the deregulation of financial services in the UK in the 1980s. Commonly known as FIMBRA, it has some 8,000 members, including most independent investment advisers.

## FINANCIAL INTERMEDIARY

Any individual or institution that mediates between savers (that is sources of funds) and borrowers (that is users of funds). The chain from original source to ultimate use can be a long one, with many intermediaries to be found along the way.

## *FINANCIAL TIMES*

The famous daily financial newspaper printed in London and Frankfurt on pink paper. It is the bible of the European financial community in the same way as the WALL STREET JOURNAL is in the USA. The *Financial Times* is owned by the Pearson Group which also owns half of *The Economist*.

---

*The* Financial Times *was founded by Horatio Bottomley, one of the most audacious swindlers of this century. Bottomley was also a member of Parliament, a job which he interspersed with being bankrupt, founding the* Hackney Hansard, *and going on trial several times for fraud. He eventually spent five years in jail.*

---

## FINANCIAL YEAR

The 12-month period covered by a company's accounts. On occasions, a financial year can be a period of less or more than 12 months. For example, when a company wants to change the ending of its financial year from (say) inconvenient May to more convenient December, it will have to have a financial year of either seven months or 19 months (7 + 12).

## FIXING

The setting of the GOLD price in London twice a day – at 10.30am and at about 3pm – by five big gold dealers. For years the five were N.M. Rothschild, Mocatta & Goldsmid, Johnson Matthey, Samuel Montagu and Sharps Pixley. Then Johnson Matthey fell on hard times and its bullion business was taken over by Westpac, an Australian bank which renamed it Mase, then sold it to an American bank, Republic National.

## FLAT BOND

A BOND that is traded at a price which does not include any of the INTEREST that has accrued (but not been paid) on it. This may be either because the bond ISSUE is in default or because the bond is a so-called income bond. With such a bond, interest is only paid if a certain level of income is achieved by the issuer.

## FLIGHT CAPITAL

Money that rushes out of a country when political or economic uncertainty undermines people's faith in the currency's ability to maintain its value. Such money tends to head for stable places like Geneva and Miami, and for stable currencies like the Deutschmark and the Swiss franc.

In the 1970s, when banks were lending huge sums of money for the further development of Latin American nations, there were on occasions larger sums of flight capital flowing in the opposite direction (from developing country to banking centre) than there were coming in.

## FLIP-FLOP BOND

A BOND that can be turned into another type of DEBT instrument at the investor's discretion, and is then equally easily flipped back again into the original form of investment.

## FLOAT

There are two meanings.

**1** The number of securities in an ISSUE that are free to be traded; that is, they are not held by investors unlikely or unable to sell them.
**2** Money that arises in the accounts of banks from cheques in the process of being cleared.

## FLOATING CHARGE

SECURITY given by a borrower to a lender that floats over all the borrower's assets. Thus if the borrower fails to repay its LOAN, the lender can claim any of its assets, up to the value of the loan.

## FLOATING RATE

A RATE OF INTEREST that changes with the cost of funds.

## FLOATING RATE NOTE

A BOND with a COUPON whose rate varies in line with a market RATE OF INTEREST. Popular in the EUROMARKET, floating rate notes (FRNS) appeal particularly to borrowers who expect interest rates to fall. At such a time they do not want to be locked into paying the fixed rates found on traditional bonds.

## FLOOR

There are two meanings.

**1** The minimum RATE OF INTEREST on a FLOATING RATE NOTE.
**2** The place in a STOCK EXCHANGE where trading actually takes place (or used to).

## FLOTATION

The launching of a new BOND or EQUITY issue on to

a CAPITAL MARKET. On all markets there are complicated rules governing the way in which flotations
must take place. Observance of the rules is
ensured by regulators such as the SECURITIES AND
EXCHANGE COMMISSION in the USA, and the COMMIS-
SION DES OPERATIONS DE BOURSE in France. The rules
add considerably to the cost of flotation. (See also
INITIAL PUBLIC OFFERING.)

## FOOTSIE
See FT-SE 100.

## FORCED SAVINGS
Savings that accrue without the consumer making
a decision to save. This can happen in all sorts of
ways: because governments levy taxes which go
towards paying old-age pensions, for example; or
because certain expenditure is prohibited, as
when restrictions are imposed on foreign travel.

## FORECASTING
The human instinct to try and predict the future is
found everywhere, particularly in things financial.
Any degree of certainty about the future that is not
generally known promises huge gains to those
who do know it.

## FOREIGN BOND
A BOND denominated in a currency foreign to the
issuer, and sold in the domestic market of the currency of issue. Thus a Swiss franc bond issued by
a Japanese company and sold in Switzerland is a
foreign bond on the Swiss market. (See also
EUROBOND.)

## FOREIGN EXCHANGE
The means whereby payments are made between
one country and another. The foreign-exchange
(forex) markets are among the biggest markets of
any kind in the world, and dealers in them have
shown time and again that they can spoil the best-
laid plans of ministers as to what should be their
currency's exchange rate.

Huge sums of money cross the exchanges every

day, much of it in search of short-term gain (even as short as overnight). Its effect on rates is at odds with the general desire of industry and government to see stability in forex markets.

### FORFAITING
Also known as a forfait, the business of discounting a FINANCIAL INSTRUMENT – like a BILL OF EXCHANGE – used to finance the export of capital goods. Banks buy the bills at a DISCOUNT, and then trade them.

The forfait market grew up in Switzerland, where it concentrated on buying east–west trade debts; but its name became increasingly Anglicised (from a forfait to forfaiting) as the market shifted to London in the 1980s.

### FORGERY
A counterfeit coin, note or document that tries to pass as something that it is not. Forgeries often involve the copying of other people's signatures.

To make forgery as difficult as possible, the printing of notes has become a highly specialised task. It involves the use of a number of technical devices, and most of the world's currencies are now printed either in the UK or the USA.

*Crime breeds in the gaps between opportunities and aspirations.*
Graffito

### FORWARD CONTRACT
An agreement now to buy a specified quantity of a COMMODITY or currency at some specified future time and place. A forward contract in the FOREIGN-EXCHANGE market might involve an agreement to buy £100,000-worth of three-month sterling for dollars; that is, to pay now (in dollars) for the delivery of £100,000 in three months' time.

The exchange rate to be paid for this sterling will reflect market expectations about the appreciation or DEPRECIATION of sterling against the dollar over the next three months. A premium over the spot rate will indicate expectations of a sterling appreciation; a DISCOUNT will indicate an expected depreciation.

## FORWARD COVER

The process of covering future payments or receipts, either by buying now (in the FUTURES markets) the currency that is required for the payment; or by selling now a receipt that is due in the future.

This is particularly valuable in volatile FOREIGN-EXCHANGE markets where fluctuations in rates can wipe out an ordinary business's PROFIT (and more) in less time than it takes to print an invoice.

---

*The essence of successful fraud is that honest people should not suspect.*
*Which honest people?*

---

## FRAUD

An act of deception aimed at gaining financial benefit illegally, at the expense of others. Fraud can be the result of many different kinds of deception, from lying in documents to back up a new ISSUE of securities, to false accounting in a company's annual reports, to pretending to be a registered BROKER, to simply forging notes. (See also SERIOUS FRAUD OFFICE.)

---

*It is estimated that the average company in the USA loses between 2% and 5% of its gross turnover in fraud.*

---

## FREDDIE MAC

See FEDERAL HOME LOAN MORTGAGE CORPORATION.

## FRN

See FLOATING RATE NOTE.

## FT-SE 100

The STOCK index introduced on January 1st 1984 by the FINANCIAL TIMES and the London STOCK

EXCHANGE, known affectionately as FOOTSIE. The INDEX started life at a level of 1,000. The lowest it has ever reached was 986.9 on July 23rd 1984.

FOOTSIE is a computerised index of 100 big UK companies. It was designed to fill a gap between the FT ordinary share index (started in 1935) which contained a mere 30 companies, and the FT all-share index which contained hundreds and was calculated infrequently. The FOOTSIE has now replaced the FT ordinary share index and become by far the most popular index of the London market. The first stock-index options and futures to be traded in London were based on the FOOTSIE.

> *The greatest rise in the Footsie index in a single day was of 142.2 points on October 21st 1987 (7.9%); the greatest fall was of 278.3 points on the day before, October 20th (13.4%).*

### FULL FAITH AND CREDIT
See GOVERNMENTS.

### FUND MANAGEMENT
The process of managing other people's money with the aim of getting a certain return on it. Big institutions, like pension funds and INSURANCE companies, spend much of their time in fund management, placing the small savings of their many customers in fruitful investments.

### FUNGIBLE
The quality of those things (like notes and coins) of which any one single specimen is indistinguishable from any other. A person owed $1 does not bother which particular dollar note he or she receives, even if it is frayed at the edges. Anything to be used as money (be it cowrie shells, beads or GOLD pieces) has to be fungible.

### FUTURES
Contracts to buy something in the future at a price agreed in the present. First developed in agricultural COMMODITY markets, like those for orange

juice and pork bellies, futures then spread into financial markets. There are now futures in Eurodollar deposits, government bonds and STOCKMARKET indexes.

There has been much competition between different financial centres to set up the world's leading futures markets. Traditional centres have not had it all their own way. In the USA Chicago has given New York a run for its money; in Europe Paris's MATIF is fiercely competitive with London's LIFFE; and in the Far East Singapore is a more lively centre than Hong Kong.

## GEARING

The indebtedness of a company expressed as a percentage of its EQUITY capital, known in the USA as leverage. A highly leveraged company is one with a lot of loans compared with its equity. (See also LEVERAGED BUY-OUT.)

## GENERAL POLICY

An INSURANCE policy that gets around a trader's need to insure every single shipment separately. The trader and the insurer agree in advance on COVER up to a certain ceiling. The trader then merely advises the insurer on the nature and value of shipments when they are made and until (in total) they reach the ceiling.

## GILTS

Short for gilt-edged SECURITY, a British term for those securities that are as good as GOLD; usually reserved exclusively for government bonds. Top-notch STOCK is usually referred to as BLUE CHIP.

## GINNIE MAE

See GOVERNMENT NATIONAL MORTGAGE ASSOCIATION.

## GIRO

A payment system organised by a group of banks or by the postal authorities. It enables the banks to make payments among themselves without shuffling CASH perpetually from one to another. A giro system transfers funds among the accounts which the participating banks hold at the giro's central CLEARING HOUSE.

## GLASS-STEAGALL ACT

A law put forward by Senator Carter Glass and Representative Henry Steagall in 1933 which was a milestone in US banking legislation. It prevents any commercial BANK in the USA from underwriting or dealing in securities. Securities business is left as the exclusive preserve of investment banks.

This strict divide was created in the wake of the financial scandals of the late 1920s and early 1930s. A number of banks had used depositors money to support the price of securities that they were underwriting, sometimes with disastrous consequences for the depositors. Today, however, Mr Glass and Mr Steagall's dividing line looks very frayed.

The act also authorised the first bank deposit INSURANCE scheme. (See DEPOSIT PROTECTION and FEDERAL DEPOSIT INSURANCE CORPORATION.)

## GLOBAL CUSTODY

A service for the worldwide safekeeping and settlement of securities. A small number of banks have managed to establish very profitable global custody departments.

## GLOBAL MARKET

A market for goods or services that attracts buyers from all over the world. The idea that there might be a global market for a very wide range of products and services (from Mars bars to mortgages) was popularised in the 1980s by a marketing professor from Harvard called Theodore Levitt.

However, many financial markets were global for many years before that.

- Customers of banks in London and New York come from all over the globe in search of trade finance facilities, or better returns in the EURO-MARKET.
- LLOYD'S of London insures risks (especially those at sea) all over the world.
- Hard commodities (metals) and soft commodities (agricultural goods) have been bought and sold at COMMODITY exchanges in the major financial centres by buyers and sellers from all over the planet for at least a century.

## GOLD

The precious metal that individuals most like to hoard when they feel uncertain about the value of money. Central banks also like to hoard some of their nation's RESERVES in gold, to the tune of about 950m oz. The biggest store of the yellow metal is believed to be 80ft below the streets of Manhattan, where the Federal Reserve Bank of New York keeps much of the world's store.

For most of the nineteenth century the UK had a monetary system based on gold (the so-called Gold Standard). Notes and coin were freely convertible into their worth in gold by the CENTRAL BANK, and gold was exported and imported freely to settle accounts between the central banks of different nations. The Gold Standard was abandoned in 1914 at the outbreak of the first world war.

One of the problems with using gold for such a purpose was that the growth in world trade was restricted by the world's ability to produce more gold, which was rather like controlling the production of eggs according to the number of pigs that are conceived.

The major problem today with supporting the idea of a wider role for gold in the international monetary system is that the world is dependent on two politically troubled countries (Russia and South Africa) for an enormous percentage of the supply of new metal coming on to the market. (See also FIXING.)

## GOLD CARD

Any plastic card (either a CREDIT CARD or a TRAVEL AND ENTERTAINMENT CARD) which offers a number of services in addition to those available from the basic card. Gold cards are aimed at high earners who are also high spenders; most require applicants to have a minimum income.

## GOLDEN HANDCUFFS

A very generous CONTRACT which persuades managers to stay with a company when they might have thought of leaving; for example, when the company comes under new ownership. The managers are handcuffed in the sense that they cannot afford to leave.

## GOLDEN HANDSHAKE

A very generous payment to employees to persuade them to leave without making a fuss, even if they have not completed their CONTRACT. Senior managers in the past have been known to write the terms of their own golden handshake.

*F. Ross Johnson, chief executive of RJR Nabisco, received a golden handshake of $53.8m on his departure in 1989.*

## GOLDEN SHARE
A SHARE with special voting rights that give it peculiar power vis-à-vis other shares. The term applies particularly to shares retained by a government after a PRIVATISATION. If the government wishes to sell off a company in a sensitive industry (defence, say), and retain control after the company has been cast on to the STOCKMARKET, it can retain a golden share. This gives the government the right (for example) to veto any takeover bid. The company is not then easy prey to any old (foreign) corporate raider passing by with spare CASH in its pocket.

## GOLDEN WEEK
A week on the Tokyo STOCK EXCHANGE which straddles two long holiday weekends; in other words an unusually short working week.

## GOVERNMENT NATIONAL MORTGAGE ASSOCIATION
Commonly known as Ginnie Mae, a US quasi-government institution designed to support the housing market. It buys mortgages, bundles them together, insures them and then issues securities backed by them. These securities, which carry a government GUARANTEE, have been very popular with American investors.

Ginnie Mae was split off from the FEDERAL NATIONAL MORTGAGE ASSOCIATION in 1968.

## GOVERNMENTS
In the USA a distinction is sometimes made between governments and government securities. Governments are securities (like treasury bills,

bonds or notes) that are issued by the central government. They are backed by the full faith and credit of the US government, which means that all its powers to tax or to borrow can be called upon to repay INTEREST or PRINCIPAL on the LOAN.

Government securities, on the other hand, are securities issued by US government agencies such as the Federal Land Bank. While these securities are usually highly rated, they do not have the full faith and credit of the US government behind them.

## GRACE PERIOD
The time between the granting of a LOAN and the first repayment of PRINCIPAL. It is also a period in many loan or INSURANCE contracts during which cancellation of the CONTRACT will not occur automatically, even if a repayment is well overdue.

## GREENBACK
Slang for the world's favourite currency: the dollar. The expression arose because the back of the USA's paper notes is green.

---

*Greed is good.*
Ivan Boesky, American insider dealer

---

## GREENMAIL
Common practice in the USA in the merger-mad 1980s. Somebody buys a large chunk of shares in a company and threatens to make a hostile takeover for the company. To buy him off the company buys back the shares at a much higher price than the greenmailer paid for them.

So disgusted were ordinary Americans with this practice that they passed legislation which imposed an onerous tax on any PROFIT made from greenmail.

## GRESHAM'S LAW
One of the oldest laws in economics, named after Sir Thomas Gresham, financial adviser to Queen Elizabeth I of England in the sixteenth century. He

noted that when a currency has been debased and a new one is introduced to replace it, the new one will be hoarded (and thus taken out of circulation) while the old one is used for transactions (to be got rid of). Hence Gresham's Law: that bad money drives out good.

## GREY MARKET
Trading in shares ahead of the official start of dealings. Shares are traded in the grey market before they have been allocated. They are traded on a basis of "when issued", denoted by the letters WI.

## GROUP ACCOUNTS
The combination within one balance sheet, and one PROFIT and loss account, of the reports of a number of interrelated companies (a group). A group usually consists of a parent company (the holding company) and a number of subsidiaries.

Group accounts eliminate intra-group transactions. Somebody just looking at the isolated accounts of a subsidiary might be misled if (say) most of the company's reported sales were to other companies in the group. In group accounts all such sales are netted out (see NET).

## GROUP INSURANCE
INSURANCE obtained by an individual as a member of a group rather than as an individual. For instance, an insurance company might offer favourable car-insurance terms to accountants (as a group), on the grounds that they drive more carefully and are less prone to accidents than the population as a whole.

## GROWTH STOCK
A company SHARE that has shown faster than average growth in earnings in recent years, and that is expected to continue to do so over the next few years. Such shares do not usually pay much DIVIDEND, since the companies involved need all their earnings for reinvestment in order to feed further

growth. Investors have to look to CAPITAL GAIN for their PROFIT.

## GUARANTEE

An undertaking by a third party to be responsible for a liability (a LOAN from a BANK, for instance) should the party to the liability (for example, the borrower) do a bunk or be unable to meet the liability on time. To be legally binding a guarantee must be made in writing.

A guarantee differs from an indemnity in the nature of the undertaking. With an indemnity the guarantor takes on responsibility in his or her own right. With a guarantee the guarantor takes on COLLATERAL responsibility; that is, the same degree of responsibility as the person he or she is guaranteeing. Should the guaranteed person die, then so does the guarantor's responsibility.

## HAMMERING

An old expression for the failure of a London STOCK EXCHANGE member firm. An employee of the exchange would hammer for silence on the floor before making an announcement of a member firm's troubles.

In the USA hammering has come to refer to intense selling pressure on a market, when investors believe that prices are too high.

## HANG SENG INDEX

The main INDEX of the Hong Kong STOCKMARKET.

## HARD CURRENCY

A currency that people want to possess, and in which are happy to denominate international transactions. Hard currencies are more in demand than soft currencies, and so they tend to appreciate in value against other currencies. The hardest major currency in recent years has been the Deutschmark; before that it was the Swiss franc, and before that the US dollar. Going back even further it was the UK pound, a currency that has for some time now been distinctly soft.

## HEAD AND SHOULDERS

A recurring pattern on charts that plot market prices over time. A head and shoulders occurs when prices move up (the left hand arm), then stabilise briefly before moving up again (the left shoulder and the head). At the top of the head they move down to the right, pause again briefly on the right shoulder, before sliding steeply down the right arm.

Serious students of such charts maintain that a head and shoulders has great predictive value. It can be quite easily spotted by the time it has reached the right shoulder, by which time it is clearly flashing sell signals. (See also CHARTISM.)

## HEDGE

Something that reduces the RISK of loss from future price movements. In a time of high INFLATION, property is seen as the traditional hedge. GOLD too is a traditional hedge, but it has not been a reliable store of value in recent years. FUTURES and options provide opportunities for investors in financial markets to hedge their risks.

A perfect hedge is one which completely eliminates the risk of future loss (thereby also completely eliminating the chance of future gain).

### HIRE PURCHASE
A combination of hiring and buying that is popular in the UK as a means of paying for high-value consumer goods, like cars or televisions. At the point-of-sale or shop the goods that the consumer wants to buy are sold to a financial institution. The institution then rents them to the consumer. After the consumer has made a (pre-arranged) number of regular payments and paid a small service fee, the goods become his or her property. A number of specialised financial institutions provide this service. The RATE OF INTEREST they charge is usually higher than that on an ordinary bank LOAN.

### HISTORIC COST
The cost of something on the day it was purchased; its original cost, as opposed to its REPLACEMENT COST, or its INFLATION-adjusted cost. Accountants like historic cost because it gives them a real figure to play with. It is not very helpful, however, to claim in a company's accounts that the value of its premises is the historic cost that was originally paid for them (maybe 100 years ago). This bears little relation to what it will cost to replace them today, or to their value in the market.

In the USA it is known as historical cost.

### HOLDING COMPANY
A company set up to hold shares in other companies. (See GROUP ACCOUNTS).

### HOME BANKING
Banking done at home by individuals via a television screen, a little black box (the modem) and a number of telephone lines. It is an idea that has

been full of promise for many years, but has remained little more than an experiment. Banks are nervous about the cost of launching such a service, although that cost should fall with the growth of optic-fibre cable technology, and the resulting increase in cheap telecommunications capacity.

---

*There is perhaps no record of a bank fraud extant of which the perpetrator was not honest yesterday.*
J.S. Gibbons, Bank of New York, 1857

---

## HOT MONEY

CAPITAL that flows to wherever it finds the highest rate of return for a given level of RISK. Hot money has no long-term allegiance to any particular investment, so it flows back and forth across exchanges and can cause wild fluctuations in exchange rates. Such fluctuations have become more and more exaggerated in recent years as more and more exchange controls have been removed, and as DEREGULATION has freed money to go where it wants.

### IMF
See INTERNATIONAL MONETARY FUND.

### IMPACT DAY
The day when details of a new ISSUE are announced.

### IMRO
See INVESTMENT MANAGERS' REGULATORY ORGANISATION.

### IN THE MONEY
A CALL OPTION is said to be in the money when it has a STRIKE PRICE below the current price of the underlying COMMODITY or SECURITY on which the option has been written. Likewise when a PUT OPTION has a strike price above the current price it is said to be in the money.

---

*A Norwegian shipping magnate, Hilmar Reksten, was once assessed for income tax at a rate of 491% of his declared income.*

---

### INDEMNITY
See GUARANTEE.

### INDEX
A statistical average of the prices of a number of things. The things may be consumer goods (as in the consumer price index), or they may be stocks and shares, as in STOCKMARKET indexes like the DOW JONES INDEXES or the FT-SE 100.

Some stockmarket indexes reflect a narrow part of the whole market (averaging the SHARE price of 30 BLUE-CHIP corporations, for example); others try to reflect the whole market by averaging most of the shares quoted on it. Yet others include stocks from only one industry or sector (an index of utilities or of mining stocks, for example).

An index is a useful way of seeing to what extent, and in what direction, prices in general are moving over time.

## INDEXATION

Adjusting the value of an asset in line with INFLATION. Not such a common phenomenon when inflation is in single figures, but something that was once a regular feature of a long-term CONTRACT. For example, in many INSURANCE contracts the annual premiums increase each year by the rate of inflation, and the benefits likewise.

## INDEX FUND

A MUTUAL FUND which invests in a PORTFOLIO of shares that matches identically the constituents of a well-known STOCKMARKET index. Hence changes in the value of the fund mirror changes in the INDEX itself.

## INDIVIDUAL RETIREMENT ACCOUNT

A special fund, set up under US tax law, into which an individual can put a certain amount of money each year, tax-free, towards his or her pension. Lump sum payments received on retirement or redundancy can also be placed into an individual retirement account (IRA), tax-free, within a certain time period.

When a pension is paid out of the IRA, the beneficiary pays tax on it like any other income. Thus the IRA is a means to defer tax payments, rather than a way of avoiding them altogether.

The IRA is part of a widespread movement to make pensions more portable, so that employees can keep the same pension scheme as they move from job to job.

## INFLATION

A systematic rise in the price of goods and services over time. Economists differ in their views of what causes inflation. There are two basic theories.

- **Cost push.** That increases in the cost of the factors of production are the main cause. This includes the price of imported raw materials, and any rise in property rents. Most importantly, it includes rises in wage costs. Hence employers argue that any wage increase above the rate of inflation is itself inflationary.

- **Demand pull.** That consumers are demanding more than is being produced, and thus pushing up prices. They can only do this if the amount of money in the economy exceeds the growth in production plus the rate of inflation.

One theory focuses anti-inflationary efforts on keeping down wage demands; the other on controlling the nation's MONEY SUPPLY.

Inflation undesirably redistributes wealth and income, hitting hardest those on fixed incomes and benefiting most those heavily in DEBT. It also undermines the basis for calculating value, and enormously complicates the lives of accountants. It is not in itself, however, necessarily a deterrent to growth. Many developing countries have combined high growth rates with high inflation.

---

*The highest rate of inflation recorded in recent times was not that in Germany in the 1930s, but in Hungary in 1946 where the 1931 gold pengo was valued at 130m trillion (1.3 x 10 to the power 20) paper pengos.*
*Guinness Book of Records*

---

### INITIAL PUBLIC OFFERING
A company's first offering of shares to the general public. An initial public offering (IPO) is frequently a traumatic experience for the company and its founders. They are often making the ISSUE in order to cash in on their creation, but they are rarely prepared for the public scrutiny that is involved.

### INSIDER DEALING
Dealing in shares with the benefit of inside information; that is, information not yet known to the general public. In some countries insider dealing is a crime, but it is a difficult crime to prove. How do you show that somebody found something out before he did a deal, and not after? This is especially difficult if the deal was done in some OFF-

SHORE financial centre where information is scarce.

In the 1980s, however, in both the UK and the USA (where insider dealing was most rampant) there were a number of successful (though expensive) prosecutions of the offence.

## INSTALMENT CREDIT

A LOAN that is repaid over a period in regular, equal instalments. Such loans are most often used to finance consumer purchases, but they are also sometimes used in trade finance.

Instalment credit differs from HIRE PURCHASE. In hire purchase consumers hire the goods until they have paid off the loan; with instalment credit they own the goods during the time that they are paying off the loan.

## INSTITUTIONAL INVESTOR

An institution (such as an INSURANCE company, PENSION FUND, BANK or INVESTMENT TRUST) that makes substantial investments by gathering together the small savings of others, and acting collectively on their behalf.

In recent years individuals' savings have been increasingly channelled through these institutions, and they have come to have great influence in most financial markets. In the UK, for example, such institutions now hold more than 70% of all quoted securities.

The institutions are stronger in Anglo-Saxon economies where pensions are more frequently funded by accumulated private-sector savings. In Mediterranean countries, like Italy, pensions are more often funded on a pay-as-you-go basis: the young pay for the pensions of the old as and when they are due. Under these conditions, the power of institutions which pool long-term savings is correspondingly less.

## INSURANCE

A CONTRACT between two parties (the insurer and the insured) in which the insurer (usually an insurance company) agrees to reimburse the insured for clearly defined losses. It does so in return for the payment of a regular PREMIUM. In essence, this is a method of transferring RISK from an individual to a larger group (the group of all those who are paying premiums to the insurer).

There are two main types of insurance.

- **Casualty.** In which there is no certainty that the thing insured against will occur. Common forms of casualty insurance are against accidents (in cars or boats or planes), against damage to buildings, and against sickness.
- **Life.** In which the thing insured against is certain to occur: the death of the insured. The only uncertainty is when. This sort of insurance is usually referred to as life assurance because the event is assured of happening.

Life assurance is traditionally sold directly by sales people to customers in their homes; casualty insurance is usually sold by insurance agents who match a customer's needs with insurance policies available on the market. Agents are widely used because the terms and conditions of different policies vary greatly and can be extremely complicated. It is difficult for individuals to shop around for a policy as they would for a cream cake. (See also ALLFINANZ.)

### INTERBANK MARKET
A financial market in which banks deal with each other; a crucial part of any efficient financial system. Banks that get more deposits from their customers than requests for loans need a market in which to sell their surplus deposits to banks that are in the opposite position. For example, banks in leafy suburban districts tend to gather more deposits than banks in the heart of grimy industrial areas. (See also LONDON INTERBANK OFFERED RATE.)

### INTERDEALER BROKER
An institution that provides LIQUIDITY to primary dealers in a market. It acts as an INTERMEDIARY between dealers, able to disguise the identity of

those who are short of liquidity, and of those who have a surplus.

## INTEREST
There are two meanings.

**1** The price of money over time. (See RATE OF INTEREST, ANNUALISED PERCENTAGE RATE, COUPON, DISCOUNT RATE, INTERNAL RATE OF RETURN, NEGATIVE INTEREST, VARIABLE RATE and YIELD.)

If the rate of interest is 8% per annum, then for someone to borrow $100 for a whole year will cost them $8, when calculated as simple interest. Compound interest involves paying interest on the PRINCIPAL and on accrued interest as well. Hence if interest is due every six months, but is only paid annually, the interest due would be 8% on $100 for six months (that is $4) plus 8% on $104 for six months.

**2** Somebody's share in property; as in "she had a 50% interest in the house".

## INTEREST COVERAGE RATIO
The number of times that a company's annual INTEREST payments can be divided into its NET operating income. An indicator of how sure the company's creditors can be of repayment.

## INTEREST-ONLY LOAN
A LOAN on which only INTEREST is paid at regular intervals until the loan matures, at which time the full amount of the PRINCIPAL is repaid. This differs from a loan where interest and principal are repaid throughout the life of the loan in a series of regular repayments.

## INTERIM DIVIDEND
Part of a company DIVIDEND paid at intervals during the year. Interim dividends may be paid after six months or (for US companies) every quarter. They are rarely paid more frequently.

## INTERMEDIARY
A financial firm (like a BANK) that takes in money

from savers and uses it to earn a return for their benefit. (See also DISINTERMEDIATION.)

### INTERNAL FUNDS
Companies have two sources they can turn to when in need of money.

- EXTERNAL FUNDS from banks, financial markets and shareholders.
- Internal funds, that is, the fruits of their own labour; cash retained in the business and not distributed to shareholders.

Companies in different countries have traditionally had very different ratios of external to internal funds.

### INTERNAL RATE OF RETURN
The RATE OF INTEREST which discounts the flow of revenue generated by an investment, so that the NET PRESENT VALUE of the flow is equal to the capital sum invested.

Internal rate of return (IRR) is much used in appraising whether investment proposals are financially viable. It does not always give the same result as using net present value itself as a yardstick. One project may have a higher net present value than another, yet have a lower IRR.

### INTERNATIONAL BANK FOR RECONSTRUCTION AND DEVELOPMENT
See WORLD BANK.

### INTERNATIONAL MONETARY FUND
An institution set up as part of the landmark Bretton Woods agreement of 1944. The role of the International Monetary Fund (IMF) was to oversee the system of fixed exchange rates which prevailed at the time.

As fixed exchange-rate systems have broken down, the IMF has found new roles for itself. It was deeply involved in sorting out the developing-country DEBT crisis of the early 1980s, imposing economic conditions on nations before agreeing to new loans and to the RESCHEDULING of old ones.

Headquartered in Washington, DC, the IMF has over 140 member countries. Originally confined to the capitalist West, they now include many of the newly converted states of eastern Europe. Each country pays a membership fee (its quota) which is related to the size of its economy. Members can then borrow up to 25% of their quota at will; any more and they have to accept certain conditions from the IMF on their economic performance. The managing director of the IMF is traditionally a European and the deputy managing director an American.

## INTERNATIONAL SECURITIES MARKET ASSOCIATION

The ISMA was founded in 1969 in Zürich. It was originally called the Association of International Bond Dealers (AIBD) but changed its name in 1991. It is a loosely knit club whose 900 member firms from over 30 countries deal in and underwrite international bonds. The ISMA issues rules and regulations, and supervises the activities of its members.

## INTERNATIONAL STOCK EXCHANGE

The London Stock Exchange changed its name to the International Stock Exchange in the 1980s to match what it saw as its new role as the premier STOCK EXCHANGE in Europe.

For many years the London Stock Exchange was second only to the NEW YORK STOCK EXCHANGE, but in recent years it has been overtaken by Tokyo. It is still by far the largest exchange in Europe, however, and it has traded an increasing volume of non-UK shares. On some days, for example, its volume of Dutch and Swedish shares has been half as much as the volume traded on the Dutch and Swedish domestic markets.

These days all trading is done via television screens and telephones. The FLOOR (where brokers used to meet market makers and scream out their clients' orders) has been converted into office accommodation.

## INTRODUCTION

A way of introducing a company to a STOCKMARKET. No new shares are issued, but existing shares (which may be in the hands of a small number of founding managers, or the members of one family) are spread around and sold more widely.

## INVERSE YIELD CURVE

In a normal structure of INTEREST rates, the rate for a long-term FINANCIAL INSTRUMENT is higher than that for a SHORT-TERM one. Plot this as a graph (rates on the vertical axis, MATURITY on the horizontal axis) and the curve slopes upwards from the bottom left-hand corner to the top right.

In circumstances, for example, where there are strong expectations that a currently high INFLATION rate will soon fall rapidly, this curve can slope the other way; the longer the maturity the lower the rates. Plotting this on a graph is said to produce an inverse yield curve.

## INVESTMENT BANK

A BANK whose main business is raising money for companies (or similar organisations) by marketing new public issues of the organisation's securities, or by placing private DEBT instruments with lenders. In the UK such a bank is generally called a MERCHANT BANK. (See also GLASS-STEAGALL ACT.)

## INVESTMENT MANAGERS' REGULATORY ORGANISATION

A UK creation that followed THE CITY of London's BIG BANG. Commonly known as IMRO, it is a self-regulatory body which looks after firms whose main activity is investment management; for example, managers of unit trusts, investment trusts, or pension funds.

## INVESTMENT TRUST

An institution that issues shares to investors, and reinvests their money in a diversified PORTFOLIO of securities. An investment trust thus gives the small investor the benefit of diversification without the enormous transaction cost usually associated with it.

For some reason investment trusts often trade at

a substantial DISCOUNT to the value of the shares in their portfolios. This leaves them vulnerable to takeover by an ASSET STRIPPER.

## INVISIBLES

Traded items that never see the inside of a container, but which earn foreign currency nevertheless. Services like banking, INSURANCE and tourism make up the bulk of a nation's invisible trade. Some countries (like the UK) have a big surplus on their invisible trade account because they are especially attractive to tourists or bankers.

Increasingly, however, the distinction between visible and invisible trade is becoming blurred. When Ford sells a (visible) car outside the USA its price includes a lot of (invisible) services, such as the company's R&D facilities, financing, and so on. When tourists go home they (usually) take a lot of visible items with them in their luggage.

## IPO

See INITIAL PUBLIC OFFERING.

## IRA

See INDIVIDUAL RETIREMENT ACCOUNT.

## ISSUE

The sale of a new SECURITY. An issue can be made in several ways:

- through an OFFER FOR SALE in which the issuing house (that is a BANK) buys the securities from the company and then sells them to the public;
- through a direct sale by the company itself;
- through a PRIVATE PLACEMENT with a limited number of investors.

A company's issued SHARE capital is the face value of all the issues of shares that it has made. Issued capital is to be distinguished from MARKET CAPITAL-ISATION, which is the value put upon all these issued shares by the STOCKMARKET (that is, the share price multiplied by the number of shares in issue).

## J

**JOBBER**
The old name for a MARKET MAKER on the London STOCK EXCHANGE. The long-standing existence of DUAL CAPACITY meant that before BIG BANG in 1986 a jobber could not be a BROKER, and vice versa. Jobbers could only deal directly with brokers or other jobbers, not with the general investing public.

Dual capacity has now been removed, as has the distinction between jobbers and brokers.

**JUNK BOND**
Technically a BOND issued by a US company whose RATING is below investment grade, a ranking given by the two dominant CREDIT-RATING agencies in the world: Moodys and Standard & Poor's. Investment grade is important because certain large financial institutions (like pension funds) are forbidden by their statutes to invest in anything that is below investment grade. That restricts the size of the market for junk bonds.

Junk can either be high-class bonds that have fallen on hard times, or high-risk bonds that start off with a lowly rating. In the 1980s the US investment bank Drexel Burnham Lambert persuaded large numbers of investors that the extra returns on junk bonds more than compensated for their extra RISK.

## KAFFIR

A general term for the shares of South African gold-mining companies.

## KERB TRADING

Trading in securities outside the official opening hours of a market. For many years the AMERICAN STOCK EXCHANGE was known as the Kerb Exchange.

## KRUGERRAND

A GOLD coin created and marketed by South Africa in the 1970s as a means to persuade investors to buy more gold. The original Krugerrand contained exactly 1oz of pure gold, and at its most popular (in 1978) 6m coins were sold around the world.

## LANDESBANK

A German financial institution that serves as a mini-CENTRAL BANK for the savings banks of a region (*Land*). Many of them have branched out from their original function, and some (like the Westdeutsche Landesbank) have become virtually indistinguishable from mainstream commercial banks.

## LAUNDERING

The process of passing "dirty" money through clean places (like Switzerland) in order to hide it from the tax inspector, or to disguise from the police where it came from (as with drug money). Laundering is often accomplished by introducing dirty money into legitimate businesses (like construction) where costs cannot always be clearly identified.

## LBO

See LEVERAGED BUY-OUT.

## LEAD MANAGER

A BANK which leads the organisation of a SYNDICATED LOAN or of an underwriting of securities. The lead manager does most of the donkey work in the negotiation with the borrower, and guarantees to take up the largest part of any ISSUE that is left unsold. For that it gets the biggest fee, and top billing on the TOMBSTONE.

## LEASING

The hiring of capital goods or equipment by manufacturing companies in order to avoid the all-at-once cost of purchasing them. A financial institution buys the capital goods, sets the capital cost off against its taxable income and leases the goods to a manufacturer. Much of the tax benefit to the leasing institution is passed on to the lessee in the form of lower charges.

Leasing is particularly attractive when:

- the lessee has used up all its available capital allowances (because of its own heavy expenditure on capital goods);

- the lessee does not have the CASH to make a straight-out capital purchase;
- the lessee does not want to be burdened with the chores of ownership.

## LENDER OF LAST RESORT

The ultimate responsibility of a CENTRAL BANK is to act as lender of last resort to a nation's financial system, typically to provide the banks under its charge with enough money to stop a run on any particular one of them.

All banks are illiquid, that is, the average MATURITY of their loans exceeds the average maturity of their deposits. Should all depositors demand their money back immediately and simultaneously, there is no bank that could meet their demands. They could not call in their loans fast enough.

In such a situation the lender of last resort pumps limitless amounts of money into the system until depositors are reassured that they will be repaid as and when they wish. In the single global market of the 1990s, however, it is doubtful whether any authority would have sufficient resources to act in this way if called upon to do so.

## LETTER OF CREDIT

An arrangement with a BANK to make money available to a customer abroad. The customer's account is debited with the required amount, and the bank then instructs its relevant CORRESPONDENT BANK to make the money available wherever the customer wants it. As a security check, the bank will send its correspondent a copy of the customer's signature.

## LEVERAGE

See GEARING.

## LEVERAGED BUY-OUT

The takeover of a company in which most of the purchase price is paid with borrowed money; that is, loans largely secured on the assets of the company being bought. Repayment of the LOAN then comes from the CASH FLOW of the company.

In the late 1980s leveraged buy-outs (LBOs) became extremely common in the USA. The biggest takeover ever – the $25.3 billion purchase of RJR Nabisco by Kohlberg Kravis Roberts, a New York firm of takeover specialists – was an LBO. In the peak year of 1988 there were LBOs worth some $60 billion in the USA. Retail chains were particularly vulnerable to them; Safeway, Macy and Montgomery Ward were all subject to multi-billion dollar leveraged buy-outs.

> *Everybody, I am confident, understands that leverage, when applied to financial matters, involves using other people's money to try to make more money than you could by using only your own.*
> Paul Sarnoff, *Superleverage*

## LIABILITY MANAGEMENT
The business of managing a BANK's liabilities (essentially its deposits). The knack is to structure them so that their RISK, MATURITY and LIQUIDITY are related to the shifting demand for loans (assets) in a way that optimises the institution's return.

## LIBOR
See LONDON INTERBANK OFFERED RATE.

## LIEN
Obtaining certain rights to property until a DEBT owed by the owner of the property has been repaid. For as long as a lien exists on a property the owner loses the right to sell it, even though he or she may retain legal ownership of it.

## LIFE ASSURANCE
See INSURANCE.

> *The highest recorded insurance payout on a single life is the $18m paid in 1970 to Linda Mullendore after the murder of her husband, an Oklahoma rancher.*
> *Guinness Book of Records*

## LIFFE
See LONDON INTERNATIONAL FINANCIAL FUTURES EXCHANGE.

## LIMIT ORDER
An order from a client to a BROKER with conditions that limit, for example, the price range within which the broker can buy or sell a SECURITY on the client's behalf. (See also STOP ORDER.)

## LINE OF CREDIT
A loan FACILITY made available to a debtor by a creditor on condition that the debtor use it to buy goods or services from the creditor. Banks also provide customers with lines of credit to enable them to make a series of purchases which have been agreed with the BANK in advance.

## LIQUIDATION
The distribution of a company's assets after it has ceased trading. The assets are divided among the company's creditors. Preferential creditors of various sorts (like the tax authorities and unpaid employees) get first priority. What is left is then divided among the rest, each according to the amount it is owed.

## LIQUIDITY
The condition (of a company or a market) which has plenty of liquid assets; that is, assets that can be quickly turned into CASH. In such a market it is easy to buy or sell (in other words to liquidate) financial instruments within a narrow (well-publicised) price range.

*As many as 30% of all US liquidations are said to be the result of fraud.*

## LISTING
The addition of a company's CAPITAL to the list of other shares and DEBT instruments that are traded on a particular STOCK EXCHANGE. The obtaining of a listing can be expensive. As a general rule, the

**LISTING** 127

higher the status of the exchange the more the listing costs. It can also involve the company in disclosing information that it would prefer to keep to itself.

## Lloyd's

A London INSURANCE market which began in the eighteenth-century coffee house of a man called Edward Lloyd. The market, which started as an association of London underwriters, has grown into a complex and unique organisation. At its centre are more than 25,000 names, wealthy folk who pledge their wealth, without limit, to underwrite insurance risks (see NAME and UNDERWRITER).

In recent years the market's considerable reputation has been tarnished by a series of scandals and heavy losses that have discouraged individuals from becoming names. Without a continuous flow of new names the market itself is in danger. To compensate for the loss of names, the market has recently introduced the concept of limited liability.

In its early years Lloyd's was almost exclusively involved with marine insurance, and it still produces Lloyd's Register of Shipping, the most authoritative listing of the world's merchant fleet, and of its seaworthiness. (See also LUTINE BELL.)

## Loan

A transaction in which the owner of property (usually money) allows somebody else (the borrower) to have use of that property. As part of the transaction, the borrower usually agrees to return the property after a certain period, and to pay a price for using it. In a case where the property lent is money, that price is called INTEREST.

## Loan stock

That part of a company's CAPITAL issued in the form of INTEREST-bearing long-term loans or bonds.

## London Interbank Offered Rate

Commonly known as LIBOR, the RATE OF INTEREST which prime banks in the EUROMARKET pay each other for interbank deposits. LIBOR is a floating rate, changing all the time.

Much lending in the Euromarket is pegged to three-month or six-month LIBOR, although some borrowers prefer to peg their rates to a domestic rate in the currency of their borrowing, such as the US prime rate in the case of Eurodollars.

## LONDON INTERNATIONAL FINANCIAL FUTURES EXCHANGE

Commonly known as LIFFE. Housed in THE CITY of London's venerable Royal Exchange building, Liffe first breathed in September 1982 and grew rapidly in both turnover and range of contracts. It has been challenged as Europe's premier FUTURES market by the highly successful MATIF in Paris.

## LONGS

UK government securities with a MATURITY of more than 15 years. They are also called long-dated STOCK.

Investors are said to be long in a stock when their supply of the stock plus their commitments to buy it exceed their commitments to sell it.

## LUTINE BELL

A bell salvaged in 1859 from the frigate *Lutine* that had been lost at sea 60 years earlier. The bell hangs in the main hall of the LLOYD'S insurance market. Its ringing is a doleful sound for the market, for it is rung every time an announcement of importance is made; in the old days these were mostly about the sinking of ships insured with Lloyd's.

## M&A
See MERGERS AND ACQUISITIONS.

## MAIN BANK
Major Japanese companies use many banks, but each has one main bank. A main bank is much closer to its corporate customer than any comparable BANK would be in the USA or Europe (with the possible exception of Germany). It has access to more information about the company than any other; it lends more; and it monitors the company closely on behalf of all other lenders. (See also CITY BANKS.)

## MANAGEMENT BUY-OUT
A takeover of a company by a group of its managers or, in rare cases, by a team of managers from outside. The managers set up a new company which buys the old one with money borrowed from banks. The banks use the assets of the company as COLLATERAL for their LOAN.

A management buy-out (MBO) inevitably raises a company's DEBT and reduces its EQUITY. Hence it is often called a LEVERAGED BUY-OUT. That makes it doubly vulnerable to an INTEREST-rate rise: first because a rise is likely to reduce sales; and second because it increases the cost of servicing the debt.

## MARCHE A TERME DES INSTRUMENTS FINANCIERS
Paris's successful financial FUTURES exchange, commonly known as the MATIF, established in 1986.

## MARGIN ACCOUNT
An ACCOUNT which an investor holds with its BROKER, allowing it to buy securities on CREDIT. The investor with such an account is called upon to pay only a certain percentage of the market price of the securities; the rest is borrowed from the broker.

This so-called margin trading can be dangerous. It got highly leveraged investors like Asil Nadir and Robert Maxwell into deep trouble in the early 1990s. Banks would lend them up to 60% of the market value of shares that they bought. (These were often shares of the companies that they ran.) Then, when the value of the shares fell, the banks would demand that some of their LOAN be repaid in order that the total outstanding be still worth less than 60% of the (reduced-in-value) shares. If the investor could not come up with the repayment, the banks would seize their SECURITY – the shares – and sell them. That invariably pushed down the price of the shares still further, starting a vicious circle that, with every turn, reduced the banks' chances of getting their money back.

## MARK DOWN
To lower the price of a company's shares following an announcement of bad news, or of bad results by the company.

## MARKET CAPITALISATION
The market value of a company's issued SHARE capital; that is, the quoted price of its shares times the number of shares in issue.

## MARKET MAKER
A dealer in securities who is prepared to buy and sell (that is, to make a market in) the securities of a particular firm or industry. (See also JOBBER.)

## MARZIPAN LAYER
The layer of senior employees in a partnership who do not share in the PROFIT, but who are an essential part of any partnership's success. The marzipan layer came under the spotlight during the DEREGULATION of the London STOCKMARKET. Firms of brokers sold out to big City banks and the like. The partners took away huge chunks of the purchase price but the marzipan layer got very little. It often found, however, that it could quickly leave its new owner and earn more from an equally ambitious firm just around the corner.

## MATCHING
The process by which a BANK aligns its assets (its loans) with its liabilities (its deposits). This alignment takes place along three dimensions: currency;

MATURITY; and geography.

A bank with perfectly matched assets and liabilities does not make much PROFIT. The banker's skill lies in judging the right degree of mismatch to maximise profit at an acceptable level of RISK.

## MATIF
See MARCHE A TERME DES INSTRUMENTS FINANCIERS.

## MATURITY
The date on which the PRINCIPAL of a redeemable SECURITY becomes repayable.

- **Original maturity.** The length of time from the issuing of a security or LOAN to the date of the last repayment.
- **Residual maturity.** The time left from today until the final repayment.

## MAYDAY
New York's BIG BANG.

## MBO
See MANAGEMENT BUY-OUT.

## MERCHANT BANK
A UK BANK engaged in corporate finance, investment banking, PORTFOLIO management and a few other banking services. Unlike a CLEARING BANK it is not involved in running personal bank accounts, or in issuing and clearing cheques.

Some merchant banks are the offspring of eighteenth- and nineteenth-century immigrant families – such as the Hambros, the Schroders and the Rothschilds – who founded them as financial arms of their big merchant trading houses.

The power of these institutions in the UK is still considerable; many become home to retired senior ministers, Treasury mandarins and heirs. Any sizeable UK company with half an ambition employs at least one merchant bank. (See also INVESTMENT BANK.)

## MERGERS AND ACQUISITIONS

Mergers between companies, and acquisitions of one company by another; also the name given to the department of an INVESTMENT BANK charged with handling them. Mergers and acquisitions (M&A) activity is more prevalent in economies with strong, egalitarian stockmarkets (like the UK and the USA) than it is in Japan or continental Europe.

The level of M&A activity is a mirror of the general state of an economy, and is determined by three things in particular.

- Confidence as to the future level of business activity.
- The RATE OF INTEREST.
- The availability of funding.

## MEZZANINE

A layer of finance that falls between EQUITY and senior DEBT in terms of its priority in a payout or LIQUIDATION.

## MIDDLE PRICE

A price halfway between the buy and sell prices quoted for a SECURITY. When a newspaper quotes only one price for a SHARE it is usually the middle price (or mid-price).

## MIXED CREDIT

More often known by its French name, *crédit mixte*, this is a mixture of trade finance and aid for the export of goods to developing countries. The general agreement known as the CONSENSUS lays down that the aid portion of mixed credits must not be less than 20% of the total.

---

*Get money, money still*
*And then let virtu follow,*
*If she will.*
Jonathan Swift

---

## MONETARY POLICY

The government's view of how to regulate the MONEY SUPPLY in order to further economic policy on growth, employment, INFLATION, and so on.

> *When two people meet to discuss money belonging to a third, fraud is inevitable.*
> Michael J. Comer, *Corporate Fraud*

## MONEY-CENTER BANK

A large BANK in the major financial centres of the USA (New York, Chicago, Miami, Los Angeles, and so on) which acts as a CLEARING BANK for smaller banks in the region. Because of this wider role, concern about the health of money-center banks is greater than it is for other banks. When they sneeze, the USA catches cold.

## MONEY MARKET

A market in which banks and other financial institutions buy and sell SHORT-TERM financial instruments such as bills and COMMERCIAL PAPER (that is money) among themselves.

## MONEY-MARKET FUND

A fund which gathers individuals' small savings and invests them in the MONEY MARKET. Money-market funds were particularly popular in the USA when US INTEREST-rate controls restricted the amount that banks could pay on regular deposits. The funds gave individuals a chance to circumvent the controls by giving them indirect access to the (uncontrolled) money markets.

## MONEY PURCHASE

A pension scheme in which the contributions are clearly defined and laid down, but the benefits are not. On the beneficiary's retirement the lump sum that has accumulated is used to buy an ANNUITY.

## MONEY SUPPLY

The amount of money circulating in an economy. At its simplest this amounts to notes and coin only (generally called M0), and ranges through M1, M2 and M3 (cash plus all BANK deposits). The higher the number, the more (and longer-term) are the deposits that are included in the measure.

## MORATORIUM

A period agreed between a borrower and a lender in which repayments of PRINCIPAL are allowed to lapse. Banks do not like to give moratoria on INTEREST payments because it forces them to do nasty things to their accounts, like increasing PROVISIONS against BAD DEBTS.

## MORTGAGE

The transfer of an INTEREST in real estate to some-one else as SECURITY for a LOAN. This transfer most commonly takes place between a house-buyer and the financial institution that is financing the purchase. In many countries such institutions are very specialised. In the UK they are called build-ing societies.

A second mortgage is a second loan secured on the same piece of real estate.

---

*I can calculate the motions of the heavenly bodies, but not the madness of people.*
Isaac Newton, on financial speculation

---

## MSB

See MUTUAL SAVINGS BANK.

## MUNICIPAL BOND

A long-term BOND with a COUPON that is issued in the USA by a municipality, county or state.

## MUTUAL FUND

An open-end INVESTMENT TRUST that continually issues new shares as it receives new CAPITAL, and redeems the shares of owners who want to sell. The capital is invested in stocks and shares by the fund's managers, who are paid a COMMISSION for their services.

## MUTUAL SAVINGS BANK

A group of US financial institutions found mostly in the east coast states of New England. A mutual savings bank (MSB) is much like a SAVINGS AND LOAN ASSOCIATION (S&L) since its prime purpose is the provision of a safe home for retail savings. The MSBS differ from the S&LS in that they are treated like banks for regulatory purposes; and they are owned by their depositors, for their mutual benefit.

Together the MSBS and the S&LS constitute the USA's so-called THRIFT institutions.

## NAME

A backer of the LLOYD'S insurance market who can demonstrate that he (or she) has a certain wealth which he is prepared to pledge to the market. Names are grouped together into syndicates, and each SYNDICATE is managed by an AGENT. The agent uses the financial backing of its names to underwrite different INSURANCE risks. The names' PROFIT is based on the NET premium income of the syndicate.

On the STOCKMARKET a name ticket is a form containing the details of the SECURITY that is needed for the registration of a new owner. The name ticket is given by the BROKER who is buying securities to the one who is selling them.

## NARROW MARKET

A market in which there is only a small supply of goods or services being sold. The expression is applied particularly to financial markets (such as the STOCKMARKET) where there is a shortage, for example, of a particular company's shares on offer.

## NASDAQ

See following entry.

## NATIONAL ASSOCIATION OF SECURITY DEALERS' ACTIVE QUOTATIONS

Commonly known as NASDAQ, a computerised information system that provides brokers throughout the USA with price quotations on a number of securities. It includes securities that are quoted on the NEW YORK STOCK EXCHANGE as well as some of those traded OVER-THE-COUNTER. NASDAQ is the main means of over-the-counter trading in the USA.

---

*When the American industrialist and fraudster, Ivar Kreuger, shot himself in his Paris apartment in 1932, the news was withheld for six hours until the New York Stock Exchange had closed.*

---

## NATIONALISATION

The taking over and running of commercial

companies by the state. The financial sector frequently has a high degree of nationalisation. In France and Italy, for example, the largest commercial banks and many large INSURANCE companies are controlled by the state.

In the 1980s there was a widespread political reaction against nationalisation (see PRIVATISATION). Nationalised industries were frequently seen as inefficient and uncompetitive. In many cases they were, but not entirely because they were owned by the state.

## NEARBY DELIVERY
See DELIVERY.

## NEGATIVE INTEREST
A RATE OF INTEREST of less than zero, a feasible (though rare) occurrence in places like Switzerland, where there is a strong currency and low INFLATION. In such circumstances banks may be flooded with deposits from abroad, in search of the stable currency. To discourage the flood the banks might pay a negative interest rate; in other words charge a fee for agreeing to hold the deposits.

## NEGOTIABLE INSTRUMENT
A FINANCIAL INSTRUMENT that can be handed from one owner to another without informing the original issuer of the instrument; for example, a bank note, a BEARER BOND or a CHEQUE. A cheque may be made non-negotiable by the addition of the words "not negotiable" between two lines across the front of it.

## NET
The amount remaining after relevant deductions have been made from a gross amount.

- **Net sales.** Total sales less amounts given as discounts, and amounts coming from goods returned.
- **Net profit.** Gross income less all costs (INTEREST payments, general expenses and tax).

- **Net worth.** Total assets less outstanding liabilities. A company with a negative net worth is technically insolvent, although it may still be able to carry on trading.

## NET BOOK VALUE
The difference between the cost of an asset and its accumulated DEPRECIATION.

## NET PRESENT VALUE
An estimation of the value today of a payment that is to be made (or received) tomorrow. The payment is discounted by an amount that takes into account the time between now and the day that the payment is due. This amount is calculated having regard to expected INTEREST rates and the degree of RISK involved in the payment.

The net present value of an investment project is the difference between the present value of the future revenues of the project, and the present value of its future costs.

## NEW YORK FUTURES EXCHANGE
Commonly known as NYFE (pronounced knife), the exchange was set up in 1979 as a subsidiary of the NEW YORK STOCK EXCHANGE. Its aim was to provide east coast competition to Chicago's growing domination of FUTURES trading.

---

*The largest single trade on the New York Stock Exchange involved the sale of 48.8m shares of Navistar International, a commercial vehicle manufacturer. The trade took place in April 1986 and was worth $488m.*

---

## NEW YORK STOCK EXCHANGE
For years the world's biggest and most prestigious STOCK EXCHANGE, a barometer of the state of health of capitalism. All the most famous US companies are quoted on the New York Stock Exchange (NYSE). At its peak the value of IBM alone was greater than the value of all the shares quoted on the Australian stock exchange, at the

time the sixth biggest in the world. Bonds, warrants, options and rights are traded on the NYSE alongside stocks and shares.

Members of the NYSE have to buy a SEAT on the exchange, and the price of seats has varied greatly over time.

The exchange was first constituted under an agreement made on May 17th 1792. Called the Buttonwood Agreement, it was signed under a buttonwood (sycamore) tree. The exchange is now situated at 11 Wall Street, and is commonly known as the Big Board because of the huge board from which STOCK prices are flashed to the floor of the exchange.

The exchange's busiest day was October 20th 1987 when 608.1m shares were traded.

## NIF
See NOTE ISSUANCE FACILITY.

## NIKKEI-DOW JONES AVERAGE
A leading share INDEX of the Tokyo STOCK EXCHANGE. It is an average of 225 stocks in the First Section of the Tokyo market.

## NIL BASIS
A method of calculating EARNINGS PER SHARE which assumes that there is no distribution of PROFIT to shareholders, just the relevant tax payments.

## NOMINAL PRICE
A quotation for a FUTURES contract during a period when no trading is actually taking place.

## NOMINEE
Someone whose name is used in place of somebody else's. To ensure greater secrecy for a Swiss bank ACCOUNT, beneficiaries of the account often open it in the name of a nominee. The nominee then passes on all the INTEREST (minus his fee) to the true beneficiary, whose name need never be known to the bank. A recent agreement between Swiss banks says that they will always try to find out who is the true beneficiary of an account

before they allow it to be opened.

## NON-PERFORMING LOAN
A LOAN on which INTEREST payments are considerably overdue. US banks consider loans to be non-performing when no interest has been paid for 90 days or more. When they pass the critical 90-day threshold, the loans have to be reported as non-performing in the banks' accounts.

## NOTE
A written acknowledgement of a DEBT, in two slightly different forms.

- **Paper money.** As in "pound note" and "notes and coin".
- **A type of SECURITY.** As in FLOATING-RATE NOTE and PROMISSORY NOTE.

## NOTE ISSUANCE FACILITY
A bank GUARANTEE that funds will be available to the issuer of SHORT-TERM promissory notes in a period before the notes have actually been issued. The guarantee usually involves the guarantor in buying any notes left unsold from the issue. Note issuance facilities (NIFS) are often rolled over (by a BANK for its customer) from one issue of short-term notes to the next.

## NUMBERED ACCOUNT
A Swiss invention designed to give depositors the last word (or, perhaps, the last number) in secrecy. In practice it is far less secret than mythology would have it. A Swiss numbered account differs from an ordinary Swiss bank ACCOUNT only in the number of people within the BANK who know the name of the account holder, usually just three or four senior executives. The rest of the staff know of the account only as a number.

At one time Austrian banks offered a competing product which they claimed was superior to the Swiss account because it offered total secrecy. Some unfortunate depositors subsequently found that to be only too true. Their accounts were so secret that, after their death, none of their heirs could find them.

## NYFE

See NEW YORK FUTURES EXCHANGE.

## NYSE

See NEW YORK STOCK EXCHANGE.

## ODD LOT

A transaction in fewer shares than is the normally permitted minimum on the market. (The minimum permitted trading unit is usually 100 shares.) The buying or selling of odd lots costs more than buying or selling in larger quantities. The difference in price is called the odd-lot differential.

## OFF BALANCE SHEET

Any transaction by a financial institution that does not have to appear on the institution's balance sheet; for example, a FIDUCIARY DEPOSIT or advisory business. Such transactions are particularly attractive to banks, which have to pay an additional price (in the form of extra RESERVES) for every extra cent that they put on to their balance sheet.

In the advertising industry such off-balance-sheet business is described as being below the line. LEASING is off-balance-sheet business for the lessee, but not for the lessor.

## OFFER FOR SALE

A proposed sale of a parcel of securities at a quoted price to the general public. The sale is usually organised by a group of underwriters (see UNDERWRITER).

## OFFSHORE

Financial business in any centre that is denominated in foreign currencies and transacted between foreigners. London is by far the world's biggest offshore centre.

## OLD LADY

The Old Lady of Threadneedle Street, the affectionate nickname for the Bank of England, the UK's CENTRAL BANK. The name comes from a drawing by the eighteenth-century cartoonist James Gillray. It depicts the prime minister of the time, William Pitt the Younger, trying to pinch the Bank's GOLD from a chest which is being firmly sat upon by an old lady. The original cartoon is still in the Bank's possession.

O

## OMBUDSMAN

Originally an independent person appointed to hear and act upon citizens' complaints about government services. Invented in Sweden, the idea has been widely adopted. For example, groups of banks, mortgage lenders and INSURANCE companies in various countries have appointed ombudsmen to attend to the complaints of their customers.

Customers who use the ombudsman's (free) services retain their full right to take legal action should they not like the ombudsman's decision.

## OPEN-END FUND

See CLOSED-END FUND.

## OPEN-MARKET OPERATIONS

Dealings by a CENTRAL BANK in the MONEY MARKET in order to adjust the amount of money and credit circulating in an economy. When a central bank sells securities it takes a CHEQUE from the banking system, and the cheque disappears into a black hole. The MONEY SUPPLY is correspondingly reduced.

## OPEN OUTCRY

A method of trading in commodities or securities where traders shout out their buy or sell offers on the FLOOR of the exchange. A potential buyer or seller for the COMMODITY or SECURITY also shouts out, and the two traders then get together to finalise a deal.

## OPEN POSITION

A net long or short position in a FINANCIAL INSTRUMENT. The situation where investors have a commitment to buy (or sell) more shares than their commitment, respectively, to sell (or buy).

## OPPORTUNITY COST

There are two definitions.

**1** What investors lose by not having put their money into the highest-yielding asset that had been available.
**2** The maximum amount of PROFIT that could have

been produced if factors of production had been put to other uses.

---

*Sarah Breedlove (1867-1919), a negro orphan who invented and marketed a hair straightener, is reputed to have been the first self-made American millionairess.*

---

## OPTION

The right to buy or sell a specific number of securities at a specific price within a specified period of time (usually three or six months). Such a right can be bought and sold, but if it is not exercised within the specified period it expires. The purchaser of the option then loses its money.

There are a number of special exchanges set up around the world solely for the purpose of trading in options.

## ORDINARY SHARE

The basic type of SHARE, with no BELLS AND WHISTLES attached other than a voting right and DIVIDEND. Contrast with PREFERENCE SHARE.

## OTC

See OVER-THE-COUNTER.

## OVERDRAFT

A peculiarly European banking service, rarely found in Japan or the USA. A credit FACILITY that allows borrowers to draw upon it (up to a limit) at their discretion. They only pay for what they use.

Overdrafts are popular because they give borrowers great flexibility, and do not compel them to borrow more money than they need. The nearest equivalent in the USA is a LOAN facility, a LINE OF CREDIT for which borrowers pay a commitment fee whether they use it or not.

---

*Follow the money.*
Bob Woodward's "Deep Throat" who helped him expose the Watergate scandal

---

**OVERFUNDING**
There are two meanings.

**1** A PENSION FUND is overfunded when it has received so many contributions that it is (actuarially) able to repay more in the future than it is contractually committed to.

**2** A government is said to be overfunded when it has issued more bonds in a particular financial year than it needs to finance its DEBT.

**OVERSUBSCRIBED**
When the number of applications for a new ISSUE of shares exceeds the number of shares on offer, the issue is said to be oversubscribed. If there are 700 applications for 100 shares, the offer is said to be six times oversubscribed. In the wild enthusiasm for shares in the 1980s it was not uncommon for issues to be 20 or 30 times oversubscribed.

In such cases shares are often allocated in such a way that everybody who applies gets a (small) minimum amount. On top of that, allocations are made according to the size of the application.

**OVER-THE-COUNTER**
An open market for securities that are not listed on a regular STOCK EXCHANGE. Over-the-counter (OTC) markets enable smaller companies that cannot afford the full expense of a major market LISTING to establish a free-market price for their shares. They also provide a useful way for a company's founders to recoup some of their investment.

OTC markets exist solely on computer screens and telephone lines; they have no physical trading FLOOR.

## PAR

The nominal or face value of a SECURITY. In the case of stocks and shares this is almost always well below the market price of the STOCK. A security is at par when it is selling at its face value.

*The highest price of a single quoted share was the $50,586 that it cost to buy one share in the Moeara Enim Petroleum Corporation on April 22nd 1992.*
*Guinness Book of Records*

## PARALLEL FINANCING

This occurs when two aid donors commit themselves to financing different parts of one project in a developing country. They co-ordinate the financing of the project between them in parallel.

## PARALLEL MARKET

A market in a particular FINANCIAL INSTRUMENT that develops outside the standard channels for such a market. For example, the market in ADRS, or the parallel money markets to be found in the EURO-MARKET.

*In the year 1881 125 new issues were sold on the Paris Bourse with a market value of FFr5 billion. At the time, all France's savings were estimated at only FFr2 billion a year.*

## PARTLY PAID

Shares on which some of the CAPITAL is still uncalled; that is, shareholders have not yet been asked to pay all that is due for the shares. Partly-paid shares are not popular with investors when they give an issuer the right to call for the unpaid part at its discretion.

## PATHFINDER

A PROSPECTUS with a rough outline of a company's history and prospects. A pathfinder is sent to potential investors in advance of a full prospectus, and in the hope of titillating their interest.

## PAYING AGENT
A financial institution that is appointed by a borrower to be responsible for paying the INTEREST and PRINCIPAL on the borrowing instrument (a BOND or a SYNDICATED LOAN) as and when it is due.

## P/E RATIO
See PRICE/EARNINGS RATIO.

## PENNY STOCK
A speculative SHARE whose price is less than $1 or £1, depending on the market. Such shares can record much bigger and quicker percentage gains than can well-established companies with sizeable share prices and no reason for volatile change. It is conceivable that a 50 cent penny stock might gain 10 cents (20%) in a day, but there is virtually no chance of IBM or ICI's shares yielding 20% in a day.

The danger with penny stocks is that they can just as easily lose 20% in a day as they can gain it. Notwithstanding this RISK, they have long been popular with individual shareholders looking for a real flutter on the STOCKMARKET.

## PENSION FUND
A fund set up by a company or other organisation to manage the savings of employees, and so on, and to pay the pension benefits to which those savings entitle them. Pension funds are among the biggest investors on the STOCKMARKET, but they have traditionally kept a low profile in the affairs of the companies that they own.

That may be changing. Pension funds played a big role in a number of recent cases where top management was removed, or its decisions reversed. However, they have not yet sought what some think is their rightful place on the boards of major corporations.

## PERFORMANCE BOND
A GUARANTEE from a BANK to an importer (often

provided by the exporter's bank) that the exporter will fulfil a CONTRACT according to its terms and conditions. Performance bonds are often used in the construction industry, particularly in the Middle East, when the buyer wants to ensure that a contractor completes a contract on time, and as promised.

Failure to perform according to the terms of the bond gives the buyer some degree of financial compensation for delay or failure to meet specifications.

## PERPETUAL
Going on for ever. Thus a perpetual debenture is a debenture that never gets repaid.

## PERSONAL IDENTIFICATION NUMBER
The number needed by every plastic cardholder in order to access personal financial details through an AUTOMATED TELLER MACHINE. Individuals are requested to memorise their personal identification numbers (PINS), and not carry them around with the card to which they apply. The more cards, the more memory required.

## PIN
See above.

## PINK SHEET
A daily publication in the USA on which are listed brokerage firms that make markets in OVER-THE-COUNTER stocks and ADRS. Pink sheets are printed on pink paper and can be obtained from practically every brokerage office.

As a result, pink has become the colour of financial information. The FINANCIAL TIMES is published every day on pink paper, and many papers around the world publish their business and finance sections in the pink, from the London *Evening Standard* to the pan-Arab *Al-Hayat*.

## PIT
That part of a trading FLOOR where a specific type of FUTURES contract or SECURITY is bought and sold,

usually with much gesticulation and shouting. Perversely, pits are raised not sunken.

### PITCH
The place where a MARKET MAKER has his stall on the floor of a STOCK EXCHANGE.

### PLACING
A method of selling shares in which they are placed with a small number of large financial institutions. A placing can be public or (more frequently) private, and is cheaper than an OFFER FOR SALE.

### PLAIN VANILLA
A FINANCIAL INSTRUMENT in its most basic form with no BELLS AND WHISTLES added.

### PONZI SCHEME
A classic con-trick that has been repeated many times both before and after Charles (Carlo) Ponzi gave it its name in the 1920s. The scheme begins with a crook setting up as a DEPOSIT-taking institution (or BANK). The crook invites the public to place deposits with the institution, and offers them a generous RATE OF INTEREST. The interest is then paid out of new depositors' money, while the crook lives well off the old deposits.

The whole scheme collapses when there are not enough new deposits coming in to cover the interest payments due on the old ones. By that time the modern-day Ponzi hopes to be living under an alias in a hot country with few extradition laws.

*Charles (Carlo) Ponzi promised to pay 50% interest for 45-day deposits based on a plan to arbitrage in the foreign-exchange markets. He took in some $7.9m. But he had just $60 on his premises when he was arrested in Boston in 1920.*

### PORTFOLIO
A collection of financial assets belonging to a single owner. A well-diversified portfolio contains

a mixture of things, like shares, bank deposits, GOLD and government bonds.

Institutions offer management services to customers who want their portfolios to be trouble-free. The institution keeps the assets somewhere safe, and carries out tasks like the collection of dividends, and the claiming of rights or scrip issues.

## POSITION

The amount of securities held (or not held) by a BROKER or an investor. Investors who own more of a particular SECURITY than they owe are long in the security; those who owe more than they own are said to be short in it. (See also OPEN POSITION.)

## POST-DATE

To add a future date to a FINANCIAL INSTRUMENT like a CHEQUE so that the payee cannot obtain payment until that date. Banks are obliged not to clear post-dated cheques until the date indicated.

## POWER OF ATTORNEY

A legally binding document that empowers one person to act on behalf of another. A power of attorney may specify that the power is for a limited range of purposes or for a limited time; or it may be given unconditionally. Use of the power of attorney is increasing with the rise in the number of elderly people no longer capable of managing their own affairs.

## PRE-EMPTION RIGHTS

The right to do something before others, as in the pre-emption right of existing shareholders in a company to buy a new ISSUE of shares before it is offered to the public. In a different type of example, somebody whose property has been nationalised may have a pre-emption right to buy it back should it prove subsequently not to be needed by the state.

## PREFERENCE SHARE

A SHARE carrying a fixed rate of DIVIDEND which has

to be paid in full before ordinary shareholders can receive a penny. Likewise, in the case of a company LIQUIDATION, preference shareholders have to be repaid before ordinary shareholders.

## PREFERENTIAL CREDITOR

In a company LIQUIDATION some creditors are more equal than others, and they get paid first. Typically these preferential creditors include the tax and customs authorities, and certain of the company's more lowly paid wage-earners.

## PREMIUM

There are two meanings.

1 A regular payment to an insurer for providing INSURANCE cover.
2 The amount paid over and above some calculated value. For example, the amount paid for a company over and above its MARKET CAPITALISATION, or the amount paid to an auctioneer (like Sotheby's) on the sale and/or purchase of antiques.

## PREPAYMENT

The payment of a DEBT before it becomes due. Some loans have a prepayment clause which allows them to be prepaid at any time without penalty (often the case with mortgages). With other loans prepayment entitles the lender to charge a fee, which is known as a prepayment penalty.

## PRICE/EARNINGS RATIO

The market price of a STOCK divided by its reported (or anticipated) EARNINGS PER SHARE. When divided by its reported earnings it is known as the historic price/earnings (P/E) ratio; when divided by its anticipated earnings it is known as the prospective P/E ratio. P/E ratios listed in newspapers are of the historic variety.

The P/E ratio is a measure of the number of years it will take for a SHARE purchased now to repay its purchase price to an investor if all its earnings are paid out as dividends.

The average P/E ratios on different stockmarkets vary greatly. In Tokyo, where investors are happier than elsewhere to receive their reward in the form of CAPITAL GAIN, P/E ratios tend to be high (often over 30). In Anglo-Saxon countries, where (higher) DIVIDEND payments are expected, P/E ratios tend to be lower (in single figures).

## PRIMARY DEALER
The limited number of US (or UK) financial institutions that are authorised to buy new government securities direct from the US (or UK) Treasury. These primary dealers are also secondary dealers in that they make markets in old government securities as well, trading them in the SECONDARY MARKET.

## PRIMARY MARKET
The market in which financial instruments are sold when they are first issued; that is, a market in which the proceeds from a sale of securities go direct to the issuer of the securities. (See also SECONDARY MARKET.)

## PRINCIPAL
The face value of a financial asset, such as a BOND or a LOAN; the amount that must be repaid when the asset matures. Principal has to be clearly distinguished from INTEREST.

## PRINCIPAL-ONLY BOND
A BOND on which there is no payment of INTEREST due. The bond is issued at a DISCOUNT, and on MATURITY its full face value is repaid.

## PRIVATE BANK
A BANK that is owned by a limited number of partners, each of whom bears unlimited liability for the debts of the bank. Private banks of this sort are popular in secretive Switzerland.

In recent years the expression has come to refer to any bank that offers services predominantly to wealthy individuals. Most large commercial banks now have private-banking divisions.

**PRIVATE PLACEMENT**
The sale of a large part of a new ISSUE of shares (or of a chunk of existing shares) to a small group of investors, usually big institutions like INSURANCE companies and pension funds. The sale is private in the sense that it is not offered to the general public, and is not sold through a recognised STOCK EXCHANGE.

**PRIVATISATION**
The sale to the private sector, by a government, of businesses that have sometimes been bought from the private sector by the previous government. Mrs Thatcher, the former prime minister of the UK, was keen on privatisation, and she converted many other countries to her way of thinking.

Despite the fact that the UK government raised more than £25 billion from privatisations in the 1980s, the biggest privatisation programmes in recent years took place in eastern Europe after the collapse of communism. Particularly notable was the programme of the Treuhandanstalt, the special body set up to privatise the state enterprises of the former East Germany.

**PROFIT**
To an economist, profit is what is left over from an enterprise after all bills have been paid. Profit is the entrepreneur's reward for the risks he or she takes.

To more practical accountants, profit is the difference between the revenue from sales and the total cost of producing those sales. NET profit before tax is what is left after all money costs have been deducted from sales revenue, that is, wages and salaries, rent, fuel, raw materials, INTEREST and DEPRECIATION. Gross profit is net profit before tax, and before interest and depreciation.

**PROFIT-SHARING**
A system that allows employees to participate in the PROFIT of the organisation that they work for. Profit-sharing schemes are designed to motivate employees without actually giving them a share in

their company. These schemes often fail because workers cannot see the correlation between their own efforts and the company's profit. Profit-sharing comes to them like manna from heaven and is something that they feel powerless to influence.

## PROGRAMME TRADING

Trading in securities, with a computer making most of the decisions. Computers are programmed to let a BROKER know when a particularly significant event takes place.

When too many computers are programmed to do the same thing at the same time (and brokers all follow their orders) the market can fluctuate violently. There is little doubt that the growth of computer trading in recent years has contributed to market volatility.

## PROJECT FINANCE

A method of financing big capital projects – like the building of a dam or the digging of a mine – that depends for COLLATERAL on the expected CASH FLOW of the project. It does not rely on guarantees from third parties.

## PROMISSORY NOTE

A legally binding promise between two parties that one will pay the other a stated amount at a prescribed future date. Often referred to simply as a NOTE.

## PROSPECTUS

A document outlining a company's future plans, particularly in relation to the ISSUE of new shares to the public. In many countries the required contents of a prospectus are laid down by law. Individual stock exchanges have their own additional requirements as well. (See also SHELF REGISTRATION.)

---

*In 1720 a prospectus was issued in London for "a company for carrying on an undertaking of great advantage, but nobody to know what it is". The prospectus raised £2,000 at £2 a share before its author disappeared to the continent.*

---

## PROVISIONS

Money that a BANK sets aside out of its PROFIT to
compensate for its doubtful debts, that is, loans
that it feels might never be repaid in full. Banks in
different countries set aside more or less money
depending on their prudence.

In the UK there are two types of provisions.

- **Specific provisions.** These are set against
  specific identifiable borrowers who look
  unlikely to pay.
- **General provisions.** These are not linked to
  individual borrowers but are based on a hunch
  about what expected market conditions might
  mean for borrowers who have not yet been
  identified.

## PROXY

A vote delegated to somebody else (particularly at
company meetings) by the person authorised to
exercise it. Often used by shareholders who cannot attend annual general meetings. A proxy fight
occurs when one group of shareholders tries to
get hold of the proxy votes of as many other
shareholders as possible, in order to force its own
representatives on to the board.

## PUBLIC OFFER

A new ISSUE of securities on offer to the general
public.

## PUT OPTION

An OPTION that gives the right to sell a fixed number of securities at a specified price (the STRIKE
PRICE) within a specified period of time.

## QUOTATION

What a company gets when it becomes quoted on a recognised STOCK EXCHANGE. To obtain a quotation it has to meet certain standards laid down by the exchange. Thereafter it will have to maintain prescribed levels of disclosure.

In return, the exchange makes the company's shares marketable by providing a price, and a means whereby buyers and sellers can get together.

**RAMP**
To push up the price of a SHARE artificially.

**RANDOM WALK**
A FORECASTING theory based on the premise that the past never repeats itself. The hypothesis is that all TECHNICAL ANALYSIS and predictions of future price movements based on past behaviour are worthless. Only theory based on the choice of random numbers is relevant.

**RATE OF INTEREST**
The cost of money over time. The difference between the rate of interest paid by banks to their depositors and the rate of interest that borrowers pay to banks for their loans is called the banks' turn.

Rates of interest are influenced by three main factors.

**1** The rate of INFLATION, which acts as a floor. Only in very exceptional circumstances can a central interest rate fall below a nation's rate of inflation.
**2** The degree of RISK run by the lender. Thus BLUE-CHIP companies will be charged a base rate plus, say, two percentage points; an entirely new electronics company will be charged several percentage points more.
**3** The demand for money. After integration of the eastern part of Germany, the demand for money there increased greatly. The BUNDESBANK had a choice between printing more money in order to meet the demand, or pushing up interest rates in order to dampen demand.

Each national financial market has its own distinctive key rate (or rates) of interest. Germany has two: the Lombard rate, the maximum rate that the German markets can use; and the discount rate, the lowest rate that the markets can use.

In the USA the prime rate – the interest rate that commercial banks charge to their most creditworthy customers – is the central rate. The prime rate of major MONEY-CENTER BANKS sets the rate for the banking industry.

In the sterling crisis of 1992 the Bank of England reintroduced the minimum lending rate (MLR), the rate at which the OLD LADY is prepared to lend money to the short-term money markets. The MLR had been the key interest rate in the UK between 1973 and 1981.

*In October 1857 US short-term interest rates stood at between 60% and 100%. In late 1992 and early 1993 one or two members of the European Exchange Rate Mechanism raised their overnight interest rates to at least 100% in an attempt to keep speculators at bay.*

## RATING

A classification of the quality of different financial instruments; an assessment of the chances that INTEREST and PRINCIPAL repayments will be made as and when due.

In the USA rating is dominated by two companies: Moodys and Standard & Poor's. Each uses a slightly different scale. With Standard & Poor's it ranges from AAA (triple A) to D (for DEBT that is in default); with Moodys it goes from Aaa to C. Borrowers whose debt is highly rated can borrow at lower interest rates than borrowers whose debt is not.

*Minimum lending rate in the UK remained unchanged (at 2%) for 12 years and 13 days between 1939 and 1951.*

## REALIGNMENT

When a currency that is part of the European EXCHANGE RATE MECHANISM is formally devalued or revalued, it is said to have undergone a realignment. The bands between which it can fluctuate are changed, and the currency is effectively fixed at a lower or higher exchange rate.

## RECEIVABLES

Money owing to a company but not yet received.

A figure closely watched by accountants and bankers.

## RECIPROCITY

The granting by A of certain privileges to B on condition that B also grants them to A. Reciprocity is a principle that has been widely applied in international banking. One nation's regulator allows foreign banks to set up in its patch if the foreign banks' authorities allow the regulator's banks on to their patch.

## RECYCLING

An expression used with specific reference to the role of banks in taking surplus funds from OPEC members in 1973/74, and moving them on to places where they could be profitably absorbed. In many cases this effectively left the banks lending OPEC's money to other countries for them to buy more oil from OPEC.

## RED CLAUSE

A clause typed in red on a LETTER OF CREDIT allowing an exporter to receive all the amount due to it, on CREDIT and (sometimes) in advance of the goods being shipped. Red clauses originated in the Australian wool trade, and they enabled well-known wool shippers to pay farmers before their wool was shipped.

## RED HERRING

A preliminary PROSPECTUS filed with the SECURITIES AND EXCHANGE COMMISSION in the USA in order to test the market's reaction to a proposed new ISSUE of securities. The red herring contains a limited amount of information, including the number of shares to be issued. It excludes any indication of the price of the issue.

## RED LINING

The allegedly once common practice of putting a red line around certain neighbourhoods and ghettoes, and refusing to lend to any potential borrower living within that area. If red lining is based on race or racial mix, then in most countries it is now illegal.

## REDEMPTION YIELD

The total YIELD on a fixed-interest SECURITY, which includes the flat yield (the declared RATE OF INTEREST) plus the discounted present value of the future CAPITAL GAIN on the security. Thus a government BOND with a COUPON of 3%, a face value of $100, a market price of $50 and three years to MATURITY has a current yield of 6%, and a redemption yield of 6% plus the discounted present value of the $50 to be gained in three years.

## REFINANCING

Paying off existing debts with new loans (which are either cheaper, bigger, or have a longer MATURITY). As INTEREST rates fall, most borrowers want to refinance their fixed-rate DEBT. In some cases banks will impose penalty clauses for early repayment. (See PREPAYMENT.)

## REGISTERED REPRESENTATIVE

In the USA a registered representative is a person registered with the SECURITIES AND EXCHANGE COMMISSION to give advice on what securities to buy and sell. Registered representatives pass on a client's orders to a STOCKBROKER for them to be executed. In return they receive a percentage of the broker's COMMISSION.

## REGISTERED SECURITY

A SECURITY whose owner has to be registered with the issuer of the security. When the security changes hands, the new owner has to inform the registrar of the change.

Every company is obliged to keep a register of the owners of its shares. In it are noted their names and addresses, the day they became shareholders, and the day that they ceased to be shareholders. The place where this register is kept (and where it is open to the public) is the registered office of the company. (See also BEARER SECURITY.)

## REINSURANCE

The practice among INSURANCE companies of parcelling out RISK among themselves. If one company takes on a large risk – the insurance of a supertanker, for example – it might sell some of the risk on to a reinsurance company. The reinsurance company will receive some of the PREMIUM, and bear some of the cost should the tanker be damaged. The original insurer will keep on its own books only so much as it considers prudent.

> *In August 1857 a cashier at the New York office of the Ohio Life Insurance and Trust Company was revealed to have embezzled almost all the assets of his highly respected employer in order to support his stockmarket dealing. The revelation started a series of financial failures across Europe, from Liverpool to Stockholm.*

## REMITTANCE

Specifically used to refer to the earnings that migrant workers send from their place of work to their families in their country of origin. For countries like Turkey and the Philippines, such earnings are a significant source of FOREIGN EXCHANGE.

In tax language, remittance basis refers to a principle used in taxing overseas income. The income is taxed as and when it is remitted to the jurisdiction of the taxing nation.

## RENUNCIATION

The decision by shareholders not to take up their rights to a new issue of securities. After shareholders have renounced their rights, the rights can be sold to somebody else. (See RIGHTS ISSUE.)

## REPACKAGING

Splitting a SECURITY into different bits (its INTEREST payments and PRINCIPAL repayments, for example) and reselling them as separate financial instruments.

## REPLACEMENT COST

The cost of replacing any asset that is wasting

over time. For companies to ensure that they have enough CAPITAL to replace old plant and equipment as and when needed, they make a suitable charge against their PROFIT every year.

## REPO
See following entry.

## REPURCHASE AGREEMENT
A CONTRACT between a BROKER and a company (or BANK) with surplus cash. The company buys securities from the broker and agrees to sell them back on a future date (a few days hence) at an agreed price. By the time the securities return to the broker it hopes to have found a long-term investor to buy them. Repurchase agreements (REPOS) are common in the USA, where up to 70% of some sales of government securities have been initially in the form of REPOS.

## RESCHEDULING
The creation of a new payment schedule for a DEBT, done with the agreement of the borrower and the lender; that is, formally putting off until tomorrow what you cannot pay today. Rescheduling has been undertaken by very large debtors (such as Latin American nations), and by very small ones (like the impoverished customers of public utilities).

The infamous developing-country debt reschedulings of the early 1980s were described at the time as being akin to rearranging the deckchairs on the *Titanic*. But they have proved a lot less pointless than that.

## RESERVES
Surplus funds that are stored away by organisations to meet future expenditure. A company's CAPITAL and reserves are the funds that belong to its shareholders, that is, an amalgamation of the original capital that they put up and the reserves that have been set aside out of the company's annual earnings.

Financial institutions like banks have to maintain their reserves at a level ordained by their supervisors. Their reserves are a first line of defence against a RUN on the BANK.

Countries also maintain reserves (of GOLD and foreign currency) in order to meet future expenditure in trading, or in supporting their currency's exchange rate. These reserves are held by the CENTRAL BANK. Currencies in which central banks prefer to denominate their reserves (like the dollar and the Deutschmark) are called reserve currencies.

### RESTRUCTURING

A rearrangement of an organisation's financial and capital structure; sometimes a euphemism for RESCHEDULING. The crucial distinction between the two (restructuring and rescheduling) is that the former is done voluntarily at the instigation of the organisation itself; the latter is done less-than-voluntarily at the instigation of the lender (or lenders).

### RETIREMENT FUND

Money set aside by a company to enable it to pay pensions that it has promised to its employees. The shadowy management of these funds received much attention after the death of Robert Maxwell, a British tycoon, in 1991. Maxwell was able to pillage the retirement funds of a public company of which he was chairman, and use the proceeds for his own benefit.

### REVOLVING CREDIT

A LOAN with a peculiar condition: as soon as one bit is repaid, it can immediately be borrowed again. A revolving credit has an upper limit on the amount that can be borrowed, but no limit on the number of times that this limit can be reached.

In the capital markets a revolving credit FACILITY (RCF) is known as a revolver.

### REVOLVING UNDERWRITING FACILITY

Commonly called a RUF, a GUARANTEE given by a group of banks to the effect that funds will be available to a borrower who is raising money via an ISSUE of securities. (See also NOTE ISSUANCE FACILITY and REVOLVING CREDIT.)

## RIGHTS ISSUE

An ISSUE of shares which gives the right to existing shareholders to buy the issue at a favourable price within a specified period of time. Rights that are not exercised can usually be sold on the open market before they expire. Almost all new SHARE issues by UK quoted companies are in the form of rights issues.

## RING

A group of investors acting in concert. Their aim is to corner a market and to manipulate prices to their advantage. The most famous ring in recent years was the (ultimately unsuccessful) silver ring created by the Hunt family in Texas.

## RISK

The danger of making a loss. Investors are rewarded for taking risks; in general, the higher the risk, the greater the reward. Investors who play safe (only buying US government bonds, for instance) are said to be risk averse.

Risk takes several forms.

- **Exchange-rate risk.** The danger from borrowing in one currency and lending in another, or of having receipts denominated in one currency and payments in another.
- **INTEREST-rate risk**. The danger from, say, taking fixed-rate deposits and making floating-rate loans.
- **MATURITY risk.** The danger which arises when payments are due in seven days and receipts are not coming in for eight.
- **Political risk.** The danger of a change of government in the country of the borrower. This change may compel the borrower to renege on the DEBT, or somehow to reduce its value.
- **CREDIT risk.** The danger which arises when the IBM corporation gives credit to the IB Mediocre corporation.

## ROCKET SCIENTIST
Name given to the highly-skilled mathematicians who are increasingly effective in financial markets as they become more and more computer based.

## ROLL-OVER
The extension of a LOAN beyond its original final payment date. Many so-called SHORT-TERM loans get rolled over so many times that they eventually become long-term loans.

## ROUND LOT
The minimum number of shares that can be offered in order to make a trade on a STOCK EXCHANGE, typically 100 shares.

## ROUNDTRIPPING
At certain times it has been possible for BLUE-CHIP companies to borrow money from banks on OVERDRAFT, and to place that money in the MONEY MARKET at a PROFIT. In theory, banks then draw that money back from the money market and lend it again to the company. That process is known as roundtripping.

## RUF
See REVOLVING UNDERWRITING FACILITY.

## RUN
The nightmare of all financial authorities, the sight of depositors stampeding to get their money out of a financial institution, or of a currency, as in "a run on the BANK" or "a run on the franc".

In both cases the run is caused by fear, either that the bank is going bust and will not be able to repay its depositors; or that the currency is about to be devalued. In both cases the fear is in danger of being self-fulfilling: the bank will go bust if too many depositors want to be repaid at once; a currency will have to devalue if too many want to sell it at once.

## S&L
See SAVINGS AND LOAN ASSOCIATION.

## SAMA
See SAUDI ARABIAN MONETARY AGENCY.

### SAMURAI BOND
A yen-denominated BOND issued in Japan by a non-Japanese borrower; the Japanese version of a YANKEE BOND or a BULLDOG BOND.

### SATELLITE BANKING
A way of organising a BANK'S BRANCH network so that it is clustered around a number of larger branches. Smaller branches provide a limited range of services; big and complicated business is referred to the larger branches.

### SAUDI ARABIAN MONETARY AGENCY
The nearest thing that oil-rich Saudi Arabia has to a CENTRAL BANK. The vast RESERVES of the Saudi Arabian Monetary Agency (SAMA) are largely invested in the short-term government bills of the USA.

### SAVINGS AND LOAN ASSOCIATION
The main provider of a MORTGAGE in the USA. The savings and loan associations (S&LS) got into difficulties in the early 1980s because much of their lending was long-term and at a fixed RATE OF INTEREST. This was increasingly out of line with their borrowing (that is their deposits) which was becoming shorter-term and, after the USA deregulated its financial markets, based on floating rates. (See RISK.)

The S&LS that survived progressively switched their business into floating-rate mortgages, and into the new areas of banking that the DEREGULATION had permitted.

### SAVINGS BANK
A BANK whose *raison d'être* is (or at least was) the gathering of deposits from small savers. At such a bank the withdrawal of savings on demand is limited. Traditionally, savings banks do virtually no business with industry, and provide no money

transmission services.

In many countries savings banks have strong local roots, either as national banks with a regional structure, or as separate regional institutions. They are often set up as mutual institutions (whose depositors are also their shareholders), and not as limited companies.

Particularly strong in the thriftier parts of Europe, savings banks have spread their wings in recent years and become more like full commercial banks.

### SCRIP ISSUE

A free handout of shares to a company's existing shareholders in proportion to their stake in the company; a CAPITALISATION of a company's RESERVES. Also known as a bonus issue.

There is no such thing as a free lunch, and there is no such thing as a free SHARE. A scrip issue is little more than an accounting device; it does nothing to increase the value of the company. After it has taken place, the shareholders' equity is worth the same. It has just been divided into more little pieces of paper (that is shares).

A scrip issue is a useful way of reducing the market price of a share that is too high (and harmful to its marketability).

### SDR

See SPECIAL DRAWING RIGHT.

### SEAQ

See STOCK EXCHANGE AUTOMATED QUOTATIONS.

### SEAT

The membership of a commodities or securities exchange, bought and sold at prices which depend on supply and demand. A seat gives its owner the right to use the trading facilities of the exchange.

*The highest price paid for a seat on the New York Stock Exchange was $1.15m in 1987.*

## SEC
See SECURITIES AND EXCHANGE COMMISSION.

## SECONDARY MARKET
A market in secondhand financial instruments. When first issued, instruments like shares, bonds and certificates of deposit are sold in the PRIMARY MARKET. Much of their attraction to investors lies in the LIQUIDITY provided by the secondary markets in which they can be sold thereafter.

## SECRECY
Financial agents have a fundamental duty not to disclose their clients' financial affairs against the clients' wishes. This duty to maintain secrecy is increasingly coming into conflict with legislation that gives tax authorities and other state bodies greater powers. These powers allow them to search premises and accounts in their hunt for information about suspected illegal activity.

Many investors prize secrecy above all, and are prepared to pay heavily for it. Secrecy is thought to be found in its purest and strongest form in Switzerland. The Swiss claim that their secrecy laws were created to protect Jewish money from acquisitive Nazis in the 1930s. Since then they have also protected the PROFIT of American insider dealers and the ill-gotten gains of Ferdinand Marcos.

*Outside Switzerland, the mere possession of a Swiss bank account, if not actually illegal, is taken as proof of a sophistication bordering on decadence.*
Nicholas Faith, *The Mysterious World of Swiss Banking*

## SECURED LOAN
A LOAN which provides a lender with the right to take over certain prescribed assets of a borrower should the borrower fail to repay. The assets given as SECURITY for the loan may be physical (like property or goods), or they may be documents entitling the holder to certain payments.

S

As a result of their secured lending, banks have ended up owning all sorts of things, from airplanes to fish 'n' chip shops.

## SECURITIES AND EXCHANGE COMMISSION

A US government agency that regulates and polices trading in the shares of publicly quoted companies in the USA.

Based in Washington and established in 1934, the Securities and Exchange Commission (SEC)'s main weapon is disclosure. It compels issuers of securities in the USA to reveal much more about themselves than issuers of securities in any other country.

## SECURITIES AND INVESTMENTS BOARD

A body created in the UK in 1986 as part of the rearrangement of THE CITY's regulation that followed BIG BANG. The Securities and Investments Board (SIB) oversees the many self-regulating bodies in the City created at more or less the same time (see also FINANCIAL INTERMEDIARIES MANAGERS AND BROKERS REGULATORY ASSOCIATION and INVESTMENT MANAGERS' REGULATORY ORGANISATION).

## SECURITISATION

The increasing use by corporations of securities markets as a source of external finance, rather than banks and similar financial intermediaries.

## SECURITY

There are two meanings.

**1** Something of value given by a lender to a borrower to support his or her intention to repay. In the case of a MORTGAGE the security is the property that the mortgage LOAN is being used to purchase. (See also COLLATERAL.)
**2** A certificate which gives its owner a SHARE in the EQUITY of a company. The term (which is usually used in the plural) normally applies to common and preferred STOCK, warrants and rights, and bonds (both INTEREST-bearing and convertible).

Ancient nineteenth-century securities on which the borrower defaulted have become collectors' items. Not only is there sometimes a remote chance that the borrower might one day honour the DEBT, but the certificates are themselves often very pretty. Collecting old securities is known as scripophily.

## SELLER'S MARKET

A market in which the seller has the upper hand; where demand for securities outstrips supply, and where prices are thus expected to rise.

## SEPARATE TRADING OF REGISTERED INTEREST AND PRINCIPAL OF SECURITIES

Commonly known as STRIPS, the practice of separating a BOND into its capital element (its corpus) and its coupons. The capital is then sold as a ZERO-COUPON BOND, and the coupons as an INTEREST-only SECURITY.

The original STRIPS dissected US government bonds.

## SERIOUS FRAUD OFFICE

A special body set up in the UK at the end of the 1980s to examine large and serious cases of suspected FRAUD. There were three main influences behind the setting up of the Serious Fraud Office (SFO).

- Concern that deregulated markets had made crookery easier.
- The complicated nature of large financial fraud cases called for a special investigative unit with specialist skills, in particular, skills in accounting.
- Fraudsters were notoriously adept at playing off one authority against another. The SFO made it easier for different crime-fighting authorities to co-operate.

In practice, the SFO was given such enormous powers that it became in danger of arousing public sympathy for suspected criminals by the forcefulness of its methods. And despite a number of successful prosecutions, it was not able to reduce by much the high cost of complicated financial cases.

### SETTLEMENT DATE
The date by which deals for the buying and selling of securities must be settled; that is, the securities must be paid for by the buyer and delivered by the seller. On the INTERNATIONAL STOCK EXCHANGE the settlement date is known as the settling day, and is the last day of each ACCOUNT. Settling day is also called pay day.

### SFO
See above.

### SHARE
A word used interchangeably with common STOCK to denote part ownership of a company, granted in exchange for CAPITAL. Shares can be traded on a STOCK EXCHANGE.

### SHARE OPTION
Part of a remuneration package designed to encourage employees to stay with one employer. Share options give employees an opportunity to buy shares in the company they work for at some future date. The price at which they can buy the shares is fixed when the option is granted and is favourable at the time, although there is no guarantee that it will remain that way.

### SHARE PREMIUM
The amount by which the proceeds of an ISSUE of securities exceeds the nominal value of the issue. In the issuer's accounts the amount appears as share premium reserve.

### SHELF REGISTRATION
A system in the USA that allows companies to file with the SECURITIES AND EXCHANGE COMMISSION (in one go) details of all the securities that they intend to issue within a two-year period. They can then

pull issues off the shelf as and when they want them without having to wait for the SEC's time-consuming filing procedures.

Shelf registration was authorised by Rule 415 of the SEC, and off-the-shelf issues are sometimes also known as Rule 415 issues.

## SHORT

Making a deal to sell securities that the seller does not yet actually possess. The seller hopes that the price of the securities will fall by the time they have to be delivered so that he or she can make a PROFIT.

## SHORTS

Gilt-edged securities (see GILTS) that are due for repayment within five years.

## SHORT-TERM

A LOAN with an original MATURITY of less than 12 months is generally considered to be short-term, but the expression is used widely and loosely.

Short-termism is the name given to the widely recognised inability of Anglo-Saxon financial institutions to make genuinely long-term investments. More than their Japanese and continental European counterparts, they are under pressure to show returns by the time of their next report to shareholders.

## SHUNTER

A BROKER who deals on two different exchanges in a SECURITY that is quoted on both; for example, in the shares of Company A on the INTERNATIONAL STOCK EXCHANGE, and in the ADRS of Company A on a New York exchange.

## SIB

See SECURITIES AND INVESTMENTS BOARD.

## SIGHT DEPOSIT

A DEPOSIT with a BANK that can be withdrawn immediately or at sight.

## SINGLE CAPACITY

The separation (once strictly observed in the UK) of market-making in securities (which was the job of the JOBBER) and dealing in securities (which was the job of the BROKER). It was rather like the distinction between retailing and wholesaling.

Single capacity was effectively abolished by BIG BANG.

## SINKING FUND

An ACCOUNT into which moneys are paid at regular intervals in order to meet a large payment that is expected at some future date, such as the replacement of an asset, or the maturing of a liability (such as a fixed-term BOND).

## SOCIETY FOR WORLDWIDE FINANCIAL TELECOMMUNICATIONS

Commonly known as SWIFT, a sophisticated communications system owned by a number of banks from many different countries. It enables the banks to send secure messages to each other, giving instructions about payments to be made between them.

Started in 1977, SWIFT is a non-PROFIT-making co-operative with its headquarters in Brussels.

## SOLVENCY

The state of an organisation whose assets are worth more than its liabilities. Solvency is not enough to ensure the financial health of an organisation. LIQUIDITY is equally important.

A BANK's solvency ratio is the ratio between its own CAPITAL (variously defined) and the deposits that have been placed with it by customers. It gives an indication of the backing that the bank has should there be a RUN on it by its depositors.

## SOURCE OF FUNDS

Where borrowers get their money from. In the case of corporations there are two sources: internal and external. Governments also have two sources: taxation and borrowing.

## SOUTH SEA BUBBLE

The INFLATION and subsequent collapse in September 1720 of the shares of the South Sea Company. These had been subjected to the most extraordinary amount of ramping, SPECULATION and illegal manipulation. All subsequent STOCKMARKET regulation and securities legislation have been influenced by the events of 1720.

The South Sea Company's shares stood at 120 in November 1719, and reached a peak of 1,000 in August 1720. They then collapsed to nothing in September of the same year.

## SPECIAL DRAWING RIGHT

A pseudo currency invented by the INTERNATIONAL MONETARY FUND in 1967 and designed to provide nations with an alternative reserve currency to GOLD and the dollar.

The special drawing right (SDR) was an esoteric oddity until it was simplified in the 1980s to become a basket of five main currencies: the dollar, yen, Deutschmark, French franc and pound. The simplification resulted in some extension of the usage of the SDR; for example, a few commercial banks began to offer loans and DEPOSIT facilities denominated in SDRS.

## SPECIALIST

A member of a STOCK EXCHANGE who makes a market in a number of companies' shares by buying all shares in the companies that are offered and selling all shares that are requested. In the USA a specialist is expected to buy and sell within a narrow price range in order to maintain an orderly market.

## SPECULATION

The purchase of a financial asset with the aim of making a quick PROFIT by selling it shortly thereafter.

In the STOCKMARKET speculators are distinct from long-term investors who stay with companies through their ups and downs. In the FOREIGN-EXCHANGE market they are distinct from genuine importers or exporters who need foreign currency purely for the purposes of their trade. They are all short-term users of the same thing; but speculators seek to make a profit from it alone while the others look for their profit elsewhere.

Although it has a bad name, speculation is essential to the proper functioning of any financial market. The distinction between it and gambling is a thin one: whereas gambling is based on choices made entirely at random, speculation consists of choices that have some basis in reason.

### SPOT PRICE
The price quoted for a transaction that is to be made on the spot; that is, the price for something when it is being paid for in CASH, now. A market where things are quoted at their spot price is called a spot market.

### SPREAD
In general, the difference in dimension between one item and another, most frequently related to the difference between a buying price and a selling price.

- In banking it is the difference between the rate paid for deposits and the rate received for loans.
- It is the difference between the YIELD on bonds of the same quality, but with different maturities.
- In underwriting it is the difference between the total cost of an ISSUE to the UNDERWRITER and the proceeds it gets from selling the issue to the public.
- It is the variety that a company has in its borrowings, or a BANK has in its loans. A good spread of maturities, for example, helps to give a smooth CASH FLOW.

### SPREADSHEET
A series of rows and columns of numbers; for example, the premiums charged by an INSURANCE company tabulated against the age of the insured.

Because spreadsheets can be extremely tedious to prepare – changing one number, for instance, may require changing them all – they have been early candidates for computerisation. Many software packages are now designed to facilitate the speedy execution of spreadsheets.

## STAG
Somebody who speculates that an ISSUE of securities will be OVERSUBSCRIBED. Stags order more securities than they can afford, knowing that if an offer is oversubscribed they will get less than they asked for, but secure in the knowledge that an oversubscribed issue is almost certain to sell at a PREMIUM to the offer price as soon as trading starts on the SECONDARY MARKET.

## STANDING ORDER
An instruction from a customer to a BANK to make a regular (often monthly) payment of a fixed amount to a named creditor. It is useful for making regular payments that do not change often, like life-assurance premiums, for example.

## STOCK
For almost all intents and purposes the same as a SHARE. Stock refers to the stock of CAPITAL belonging to a company, that is, common stock, preferred stock, and so on. Shareholders are people with a share in this stock. They are also the owners of common stock.

## STOCKBROKER
A member of a STOCK EXCHANGE who is authorised to deal in securities. Stockbrokers charge a COMMISSION, usually related to the volume of deals involved, for their services. Hence when stockmarkets are busy and trading volumes high, brokers do well.

Most stockbrokers were once proudly independent family businesses. However, the great majority of them have by now either gone bust or been absorbed by large financial conglomerates. (See also REGISTERED REPRESENTATIVE.)

## STOCK DIVIDEND

The payment of STOCK in lieu of a cash DIVIDEND. With a 5% stock dividend, shareholders receive five new shares for every 100 that they already own. If these are newly issued shares, the stock dividend gives shareholders nothing. It is more in the nature of a SCRIP ISSUE.

*Amsterdam claims to be the oldest stock exchange in the world. It began trading in the shares of the United East India Company in 1602.*

## STOCK EXCHANGE

The physical place where securities are bought and sold. Stock exchanges are often found in rather grand nineteenth-century buildings in the centre of capital cities. The actual dealing takes place on the FLOOR of the exchange, although more and more dealing is done by brokers sitting in their offices and communicating via a VDU and a telephone line. As that trend continues, stock exchanges become more like offices and less like markets.

## STOCK EXCHANGE AUTOMATED QUOTATIONS

Commonly known as SEAQ, an electronic trading network for UK securities which has a continuously updated database of prices and trading volumes, and a system that allows its subscribers to deal via their screens.

SEAQ International trades in non-UK securities.

## STOCKMARKET

An organised market in securities. The 1980s saw great growth in stockmarkets around the world, in both developing and developed countries (the MARKET CAPITALISATION of Japan's stockmarkets, for example, rose from $380 billion in 1980 to $4,390 billion in 1989). As an indication of the growth in developing countries, by the end of the decade the Taiwan stockmarket was bigger than both the Canadian and the Dutch markets.

## STOCK SPLIT

The issuing of free extra shares to existing share-holders according to some fixed proportion; two for three, for example. This is no gesture from Santa Claus. It merely makes more shares represent a fixed stake in the company. What was represented by three shares is, post-split, represented by five. (See also SCRIP ISSUE.)

## STOP ORDER

An order to a STOCKBROKER to sell (or buy) shares in the future when they reach a particular specified price, called the stop price. Such an order is given by a client with the intention of protecting an existing PROFIT, or of limiting a future loss.

Suppose shares are bought at $1; they rise to $5. Everybody says sell, but the owner thinks they might rise higher. So he or she hangs on to them but gives a stop order to the broker to sell should they fall to $4, thus protecting $3 per SHARE of the gain.

## STRADDLE

The purchase by a speculator of an equal number of PUT OPTIONS and CALL OPTIONS on the same underlying SECURITY. If the speculator can get a perfect match then he reduces all his RISK, and ceases to be a speculator as well.

## STREET NAME

The registration of shares in the name of a BROKER, and without the real owner taking physical delivery of them. This use of a street name makes it easier subsequently to sell the securities, since they are held physically in the broker's custody. They do not have to be shipped back and forth to each new owner.

## STRIKE PRICE

Sometimes called the exercise price or basis price. The price, in contracts for PUT OPTIONS and CALL OPTIONS, at which the OPTION can be exercised. (See also IN THE MONEY.)

## STRIPS
See SEPARATE TRADING OF REGISTERED INTEREST AND PRINCIPAL OF SECURITIES.

### SUBORDINATED
A LOAN or SECURITY with an inferior claim to repayment compared with straightforward loans and securities.

### SUPPLIER CREDIT
A LOAN to an importer guaranteed by the EXPORT-CREDIT agency of the country of the exporter (up to a certain percentage of the purchase price of the goods being imported).

### SURRENDER VALUE
What is received when a fixed-term investment (like a life INSURANCE policy) is cashed in early.

### SUSPENSE ACCOUNT
A sort of dustbin ACCOUNT into which payments are shunted temporarily while in transit from one institution to another, or when there is doubt about their rightful destination.

### SWAP
A transaction in which two parties exchange financial assets. For example, central banks have an arrangement whereby, if they need to support their currencies, one CENTRAL BANK will swap some of its own currency for a loan from another central bank, denominated in its currency. The first such swap was for $50m in 1962 between the Federal Reserve Board of the USA and the Banque de France.

With an INTEREST-rate swap a borrower who has raised, say, Swiss francs, swaps the interest payments on this LOAN with those of another borrower who has raised, say, US dollars. This can be to the benefit of both parties.

## SWIFT
See SOCIETY FOR WORLDWIDE FINANCIAL TELECOMMUNICATIONS.

## SYNDICATE

A group of institutions (often financial) that get together to carry out some project that each would not be willing to undertake on its own. A syndicate of LLOYD'S underwriters might get together to cover a particularly large INSURANCE risk; a syndicate of bankers might make a multi-million-dollar LOAN to a developing country. The legal documentation required to bind such syndicates together is invariably extensive and expensive.

## SYNDICATED LOAN

A single LOAN that is shared among a large number of lenders, usually because it is too big for any one institution to take on by itself. Much of the international lending in the EUROMARKET is syndicated in this way.

T

## T&E CARD
See TRAVEL AND ENTERTAINMENT CARD.

## TAP STOCK
A UK government BOND issue which is sold in dribs and drabs, not all at once.

---

*The biggest fiscal surplus ever recorded by a government was the $8.4 billion notched up by the USA in 1947/48.*

---

## TAX LOSS
Any loss which a company can transfer to another accounting period and set off against PROFIT. The ability to carry such losses forward (and backwards against previous accounting periods' profit) differs from country to country.

## TAX SHELTER
Any activity which provides a taxpayer with the opportunity to shelter otherwise taxable income from liability to tax. In certain cases charitable giving is a tax shelter. Investment in activities that are considered socially desirable (like forestry or anti-pollution devices) is also sometimes given the status of a tax shelter.

## TECHNICAL ANALYSIS
The sort of number-crunching relied upon by believers in CHARTISM: the use of detailed analyses of past price movements and turnover in stock-markets as a basis for predictions about the future demand for shares. Technical analysts largely ignore the underlying business of the companies whose shares they are analysing.

## TECHNICAL RALLY
A surge in SHARE (or COMMODITY) prices due to technical reasons. These may arise because the TECHNICAL ANALYSIS spots, for example, that a certain market INDEX has support levels at which it tends to stay fixed. Or it may be something to do with the way the market itself operates; for exam-

ple, London market prices tend to move erratically on the day before the SETTLEMENT DATE. (See also TRIPLE WITCHING HOUR.)

## TELERATE

A widely used screen-based securities information service.

## TENDER OFFER

A method of selling securities developed by the UK government, and now used all over the world. The seller sets a price (the tender price) at which it is prepared to sell the securities. Offers are invited, and applicants state what price they are prepared to pay; nothing below the tender price is acceptable. After a certain time the securities go to the highest bidder. Should not enough bids above the tender price be received the offer lapses, and the whole ISSUE can then be withdrawn.

## TERM LOAN

A LOAN granted for a pre-determined length of time, typically between two and ten years. A five-year loan is a term loan; an OVERDRAFT is not.

## TERMINAL BONUS

An extra discretionary amount that may be paid by an INSURANCE company when a "with profits" insurance policy expires, or when the policy-holder dies. A with profits policy is one which is entitled to share in any surplus shown in a valuation of the insurer's relevant fund.

## THRIFT

A general expression for those financial institutions in the USA that have the word savings as the first or second word in their generic title, like SAVINGS AND LOAN ASSOCIATION or MUTUAL SAVINGS BANK. An institution whose primary purpose is the encouragement of thrift.

## TIME DEPOSIT
See DEPOSIT.

## TIP SHEET
A publication designed for private individual shareholders which tips hot stocks, rather like a racing paper tips horses. The more influential tip sheets can noticeably move markets.

## TOKYO STOCK EXCHANGE
The main market place for the buying and selling of Japanese stocks, and the second-biggest STOCK-MARKET in the world (after the NEW YORK STOCK EXCHANGE) in terms of its market value. In terms of the volume of shares sold per year, it exceeds even New York.

Stocks and shares have a rather different role in Japanese financial affairs than they have in Europe and the USA. Companies are not so dependent on them for CAPITAL; their bankers and their own resources are more important providers of funds. Shareholders are not fed with generous dividends; they have to rely for their reward on CAPITAL GAIN. One result of this is that the stockmarket is even more like a casino than Wall Street.

The Tokyo stockmarket is divided into two sections: the First Section and the Second Section. The requirements for companies to obtain a LISTING on the Second Section are less stringent than those required for the First Section. All major Japanese multinationals are listed on the First Section.

## TOMBSTONE
An advertisement placed in a financial newspaper or magazine to announce the completion of a SYNDICATED LOAN or a new ISSUE of securities. It is called a tombstone because it consists of little more than a list of names and dates. The names are those of the borrower (who pays for the tomb-stone) and of the financial institutions which participated in the deal. They are ordered in strict seniority, the size of the typeface indicating their importance in the deal. Within the same rank participants are listed strictly alphabetically.

The more the tombstones, the less dead the market.

## TONTINE
See ANNUITY.

## TRANCHE
A lump of a LOAN doled out by a lender to a borrower. Tranche most commonly refers to the chunks in which the INTERNATIONAL MONETARY FUND hands out its loans to member countries. Release of the next IMF tranche is dependent on a borrower achieving pre-agreed economic targets.

## TRANSFERABLE CREDIT
A trade credit in which an importer opens a LETTER OF CREDIT in favour of an AGENT (or middle man) who then has it transferred to the exporter. This allows the agent to be the importer without putting up the CAPITAL necessary to fund the deal. It also enables the agent to keep the identities of the importer and exporter hidden from each other.

## TRANSFER AGENT
An institution which transfers shares from one owner to another on behalf of the company that has issued them. A transfer agent also keeps a record of a company's shareholders, which acts as a back-up to the company's own register.

## TRAVEL AND ENTERTAINMENT CARD
Not quite the same as a CREDIT CARD. Travel and entertainment (T&E) cards are plastic slivers issued by the likes of American Express and Diners Club. They give the holder virtually unlimited capacity to purchase goods, but they do not give CREDIT. All bills have to be paid in full on receipt of the card company's statement at the end of each month.

T&E cards charge an annual fee to the cardholder and have a more up-market image than credit cards. They tend to be used to pay big-ticket hotel and airline bills, and are given by many corporations to their globe-trotting executives.

## TRAVELLER'S CHEQUE

A clever method of payment for travellers that was invented towards the end of the nineteenth century. It relies on a double signature for security: the owner signs once when he or she buys the cheque at home, and again when it is cashed abroad. The payer only has to check that the signatures match.

The traveller's cheque has also proved useful for internal use within countries that have a poor banking system (as in parts of Africa, for example), or that are too large to have a single nationwide payments system (like the USA).

The issuers of traveller's cheques make a small charge per cheque for their services. Most of the benefit to the issuer, however, comes from the fact that cheques are paid for, on average, 2–3 months before they are cashed. The issuing institution has the use of the chequeholder's money for all that time, at no cost.

## TREASURY BILL

A short-term instrument issued by a government, usually with a MATURITY of three months. Treasury bills are traditionally sold at a DISCOUNT, and their YIELD is a leading indicator of INTEREST-rate trends. In the UK banks are the biggest holders of T-bills (as they are called); in the USA treasury bills are much more widely held.

## TRIPLE WITCHING HOUR

That time when the expiry dates of three types of US financial instrument coincide:

- STOCK index FUTURES contracts;
- options on those contracts; and
- options on individual stocks in the INDEX.

Such simultaneity can move markets dramatically.

## TRUSTEE

A person who is entrusted with property belonging to someone else. The purest form of trustee –

one who has absolutely no beneficial INTEREST in the property – is called a naked trustee.

A trustee can act in many different roles.

- As the person charged with disposing of a dead person's property according to a will.
- As the person charged with looking after the interests of a minor until he or she comes of age.
- As the person charged with looking after money donated to a charity.
- Even, as in the case of *The Economist*, a person charged with looking after the editorial integrity and independence of a newspaper or magazine.

## TWO-WAY MARKET

A market which is as free for buyers as it is for sellers. With securities, a two-way market is one in which brokers are as willing to sell a SECURITY at its quoted selling price as they are to buy it at its quoted buying price.

## UCITS

See following entry.

## UNDERTAKINGS FOR COLLECTIVE INVESTMENTS IN TRANSFERABLE SECURITIES

Commonly known by its acronym UCITS, Eurospeak for MUTUAL FUND. The European Community has passed a special law authorising the sale of UCITS throughout the Community, believing that it is the most likely financial product to become rapidly pan-European.

## UNDERWRITER

Most commonly an institution that commits itself (usually in association with a group of other institutions) to buying up the whole of a new ISSUE of securities for subsequent resale to the public, and for a fee. The difference between the price that the underwriters pay for the issue and the price at which they sell it to the public is their PROFIT, known as the underwriting spread.

If the public is subsequently not too keen on the issue (or if the market suddenly turns against them), underwriters can be left nursing huge losses.

The term originated in the seventeenth century when underwriters wrote their names at the bottom of INSURANCE policies, thus guaranteeing to provide COVER according to the terms of the policy. The LLOYD'S insurance market still works with a similar system of underwriters.

## UNIT TRUST

The name for a MUTUAL FUND in the UK and in a number of other English-speaking countries. A vehicle for pooling the small investments of several people into a managed fund. A unit trust differs from an INVESTMENT TRUST in that every time more money is put into a unit trust, more units (shares) are created. The only way to buy into an investment trust is to buy its existing shares.

Unit trusts are designed to give small investors an interest in a PORTFOLIO of investments. But unit trusts have themselves become very specialised, so much so that the investor now has to think about investing in a portfolio of unit trusts.

*The first company to record sales of over $1 billion was US Steel in 1917. It was also the first company to have assets of over $1 billion on its formation (through merger) in 1902.*

## UNITARY TAX
A system of taxing corporations based on a calculation of that proportion of a company's business that is done in the tax authority's jurisdiction, rather than on the (more usual) basis of the profits earned in the jurisdiction. The most notable proponent of unitary tax is the state of California.

## UNIVERSAL BANK
A BANK that is able to do almost any type of financial business, from underwriting an ISSUE of securities to straight lending and DEPOSIT-taking. Universal banks are very strong in Germany and Switzerland, and (because they prefer to be lenders rather than underwriters) are blamed for the relatively puny size of the German STOCKMARKET.

## UNLISTED SECURITIES MARKET
The INTERNATIONAL STOCK EXCHANGE's second-tier market, set up in 1980. The unlisted securities market (USM) aims to help smaller, less mature companies to gain access to the capital markets without going through the expense and effort of getting a full LISTING on the major exchange. For many entrepreneurs the USM is the only means to cash in on the value of their stake in companies that they founded. However, the market was so little used in the early 1990s that it became in danger of extinction.

## UNSECURED
Without specific SECURITY against assets. An unsecured LOAN has to wait until all secured creditors have been paid before it can get anything back from the LIQUIDATION of a debtor.

# U

*All people are most credulous when they are most happy.*
Walter Bagehot

## USE OF FUNDS

An accounting statement of the flow of funds in and out of a company during the year. In some countries such statements are a legal requirement; in others they are voluntary. (See also SOURCE OF FUNDS.)

## USM

See UNLISTED SECURITIES MARKET.

## USURY

The charging of an exorbitant RATE OF INTEREST. Nowadays all developed countries have legislation to protect borrowers from usury.

- Most states in the USA have laws which limit the amount of interest that can be charged. The limits vary according to the type of lender and the type of LOAN. Some federal laws allow the limits to be broken under special circumstances.
- In the UK anti-usury laws can be traced back to the time of King Henry VIII. At one stage in the nineteenth century anything over 48% a year was, *prima facie*, considered to be usurious.
- In continental Europe the concept is also embedded in law, as part of a CONTRACT in which an evident disproportion between the power of the parties has resulted in an exploitative interest rate charged by the one on the other.

## VARIABLE RATE

A RATE OF INTEREST that varies in line with some benchmark (like LIBOR). Variable rate is American for floating rate, and the opposite of fixed rate.

## VENTURE CAPITAL

Money put up by financial institutions or wealthy individuals to back risky commercial ventures (often high-tech ones). This can either be at the beginning of the venture's life (when the money is known as start-up capital), or it can be later in its life (to rescue it, or to attempt to turn it round). For the high degree of risk involved, the investor expects a higher than average return from such ventures.

## VOLATILITY

Often used to refer to the size and frequency of fluctuations in the price of a SECURITY, or in a STOCKMARKET index.

The BETA coefficient is a specific measure of a US STOCK's volatility vis-à-vis a base figure: the Standard & Poor's 500 Stock Index. It measures the variance of the stock's price relative to the variance of the INDEX. The index itself has a beta coefficient of one; any stock with a coefficient greater than one is more volatile than the market as a whole.

---

*In the nineteenth century Walter Watts became a major figure in London's theatreland, buying two theatres with money stolen from the Globe Insurance Company. After a few flamboyant years, he ended up in Newgate prison where he committed suicide.*

---

## WALL STREET JOURNAL

The most successful US business newspaper, a daily that is owned by the Dow Jones company, creator of the main INDEX for the NEW YORK STOCK EXCHANGE. The *Wall Street Journal* is one of the few US papers to be truly national with a readership stretching from Miami to Seattle.

The paper has a very distinctive format; the only illustrations are thumbnail sketches of individuals. It is particularly well-known for several things.

- Its excellent front-page news digest.
- Its bizarre front-page articles, which cover stories that are way outside mainstream news.
- Its unsubtle tub-thumping editorials.

The newspaper has attempted to become international. In recent years it has launched an Asian edition (the *Asian Wall Street Journal*) and the *Wall Street Journal Europe*. Excellent as these products are, they have not yet taken their markets by storm. The *Wall Street Journal*'s idiosyncratic style has yet to prove that it travels well.

## WAREHOUSING

Disguising the purchase of shares in a company by using a NOMINEE and others to buy stakes. These can then act in concert to make a surprise takeover bid.

Many countries try to reduce the chances of this sort of surprise attack by regulating CONCERT PARTY behaviour and by insisting that all substantial holdings of quoted companies be declared to the public. (In the UK any stake above 3% has to be declared under normal circumstances, and any stake of over 1% during a takcover battle.)

## WARRANT

A certificate authorising the holder to buy a specified number of shares in a company at a named price, and within a specified period of time. This is similar to a RIGHTS ISSUE, except that the period of time in which a warrant can be exercised is much longer. Securities are often said to come with warrants attached.

A warrant is also a written instruction that makes legal a payment that would otherwise be illegal.

## WHITE KNIGHT

An investor who appears from out of the blue to rescue a company that is about to fall into the hands of an unwelcome suitor. In practice, white knights rarely charge out of the blue; they are persuaded by a company that is subject to a takeover battle to come to its rescue.

## WITHHOLDING TAX

Any tax that is withheld at source, that is, before the taxpayer has seen the income or CAPITAL to which the tax applies. Withholding taxes are frequently imposed on BOND interest and dividends, and sometimes on bank INTEREST too. They are very attractive to governments because they reduce the potential for tax evasion.

A DOUBLE TAXATION AGREEMENT between countries usually goes to some lengths to ensure that taxpayers are not charged twice on income from which tax has been withheld.

## WITH RECOURSE

A BANK that discounts a BILL OF EXCHANGE for a customer may do so with recourse, that is, with the bank retaining the right to claim the amount of the bill from the customer if it is not honoured at MATURITY.

## WORKING CAPITAL

What is left over from a company's paid-up CAPITAL and RESERVES after all its fixed assets have been paid for; that is, what is left for the day-to-day running of the business. Working capital is needed to bridge the gap between the time when it is decided to produce a product or service, and the time that the company receives payment for its first sale.

## WORLD BANK

The common name for the International Bank for Reconstruction and Development (IBRD), the sister organisation of the INTERNATIONAL MONETARY FUND. The World Bank has its headquarters right across the road from the IMF, on Washington's H Street.

The Bank was originally designed to help countries rebuild their economies after the second world war. Set up in 1944 as part of the Bretton Woods agreement, it provides long-term loans (usually for 15–20 years) to governments and government organisations. To fund its lending it borrows on BOND markets around the world at very fine rates.

It has two specialist sibling organisations: the International Development Association (IDA), and the International Finance Corporation (IFC).

## WRITER

A person who issues an OPTION. The individual who at the end of the day has to buy or sell the asset on which the option is written, should whoever holds the option wish to exercise it.

## YANKEE BOND

A BOND issued in a US capital market by a non-US borrower.

## YEARLING

In the UK, a one-year SECURITY issued (usually) by a local authority.

## YELLOW SHEET

A daily publication in the USA that is to bonds what the PINK SHEET is to stocks; a list of prices and firms in the market for OVER-THE-COUNTER corporate bonds.

## YIELD

The annual income in dividends or INTEREST from a SECURITY, expressed as a percentage of the market price of the security. Thus a BOND with a face value of $100, a COUPON of 10% and a market price of $50, has a yield of 20%.

- Earnings yield is the rate of return to share-holders if all their company's earnings were distributed as dividends.
- The yield gap is the difference between the yield on a reputable INDEX of equities and the yield on bonds, as measured by a standard gilt-edged government bond. This is usually positive since equities are more risky than bonds (and there-fore more rewarding). On occasions, however, the yield on bonds is higher than on equities, and there is then said to be a reverse yield gap.

(See also INVERSE YIELD CURVE and REDEMPTION YIELD.)

## YIELD TO MATURITY

The same as REDEMPTION YIELD; that yield which takes into account the PREMIUM or DISCOUNT (above or below its face value) that there is in the purchase price of a fixed-interest SECURITY.

*If he wins he pockets it; if he loses he does not pay.*
*That is known, people are resigned to it.*
Emile Zola, *L'Argent*

## ZERO-COUPON BOND

A SECURITY bought and sold in the SECONDARY MARKET at a DISCOUNT to its face value because it carries no COUPON, that is, it pays no INTEREST to the bondholder. The purchaser gets its PROFIT from the gradual increase in the security's market price over time, as it moves towards its face value, which is repayable on MATURITY.

Zero-coupon bonds are also known as zeroes.

# Part 3

# APPENDIXES

## 1  Standard and Poors' rating system

| Rating | Characteristics |
| --- | --- |
| **AAA (triple A)** | **Prime grade.** Triple A bonds represent the highest degree of protection of both principal and interest. |
| **AA** | **Highly secure.** The majority differ from AAA bonds only to a small degree. |
| **A** | **Upper medium grade.** Considerable investment strength but not entirely free from adverse changes in economic and trade conditions. |
| **BBB** | **Medium grade.** Some speculative elements. Adequate asset cover and earnings but more responsive to business conditions than to interest rates. |
| **BB** | **Lower to medium grade.** Interest is normally earned but deficit operations are possible. |
| **B** | **Speculative investment.** Payment of interest cannot be assured under difficult economic conditions. |
| **CCC–CC** | **Outright speculation.** |
| **C** | Category reserved for income bonds on which no interest is being paid. |
| **DDD–D** | Bonds are in default of interest payments and principal is at risk. Range between DDD and D indicates relative salvage values of the bond. |

*Note:* Investment grade is defined as borrowers with ratings of AAA to BB.

## 2 World government bond markets, 1992

| Country | % |
| --- | --- |
| USA | 51 |
| Japan | 17 |
| Italy | 7 |
| France | 6 |
| Germany | 5 |
| Canada | 3 |
| UK | 2 |
| Other | 9 |

*Source:* Salomon Brothers.

## 3 Investors in the US corporate bond market, 1992

| Investor | % |
| --- | --- |
| Life assurance companies | 34 |
| Foreign investors | 14 |
| Public pension funds | 11 |
| Private pension funds | 10 |
| Mutual funds | 9 |
| Households | 7 |
| Other insurance companies | 6 |
| Commercial banks | 5 |
| Savings banks | 2 |
| Broker/dealers | 2 |

*Source:* Federal Reserve.

## 4 Pension funds – asset allocation, end 1991 (%)

| | Domestic equities | International equities | Property | Cash | Domestic bonds | International bonds |
|---|---|---|---|---|---|---|
| UK | 54 | 20 | 7 | 7 | 10 | 2 |
| Japan | 26 | 8 | 1 | 15 | 43 | 7 |
| Germany | 10 | 1 | 12 | 8 | 67 | 2 |
| USA | 47 | 5 | 5 | 5 | 38 | 0 |

*Source:* Phillips & Drew Fund Management.

## 5 Share ownership in Britain, 1963–92 (%)

| | 1963 | 1969 | 31 December 1975 | 31 December 1981 | 1989 | 1990 | 1 January 1992 |
|---|---|---|---|---|---|---|---|
| Individuals and unincorporated businesses | 54.0 | 47.4 | 37.5 | 28.2 | 20.8 | 20.5 | 20.0 |
| Non-profit making bodies | 2.1 | 2.1 | 2.3 | 2.2 | 2.1 | 1.6 | 2.2 |
| Public sector | 1.5 | 2.6 | 3.6 | 3.0 | 2.0 | 2.0 | 1.2 |
| Banks | 1.3 | 1.7 | 0.7 | 0.3 | 0.7 | 0.7 | 0.2 |
| Insurance companies | 10.0 | 12.2 | 15.9 | 20.5 | 18.5 | 20.4 | 20.7 |
| Pension funds | 6.4 | 9.0 | 16.8 | 26.7 | 30.5 | 31.4 | 31.1 |
| Unit trusts | 1.3 | 2.9 | 4.1 | 3.6 | 5.9 | 6.1 | 5.7 |
| Other financial institutions | 11.3 | 10.1 | 10.5 | 6.8 | 3.1 | 2.7 | 2.8 |
| Industrial & commercial companies | 5.1 | 5.4 | 3.0 | 5.1 | 3.8 | 2.8 | 3.3 |
| Overseas | 7.0 | 6.6 | 5.6 | 3.6 | 12.7 | 11.8 | 12.8 |

*Source:* Share Register Surveys.

## 6 Capital appreciation of stockmarkets, 1989–92 (annual % change[a])

| Country | Market capitalisation ($ bn) | 1989 | 1990 | 1991 | 1992 | 1982–92 |
|---|---|---|---|---|---|---|
| USA | 4,758 | 27 | -6 | 27 | 4 | 203 |
| Japan | 2,399 | 1 | -36 | 8 | -22 | 318 |
| UK | 839 | 18 | 6 | 12 | -7 | 249 |
| France | 351 | 34 | -15 | 16 | 1 | 547 |
| Germany | 348 | 44 | -11 | 6 | -12 | 263 |
| Canada | 243 | 21 | -15 | 8 | -14 | 67 |
| Switzerland | 195 | 24 | -7 | 14 | 16 | 279 |
| Hong Kong | 172 | 3 | 4 | 43 | 27 | 519 |
| Netherlands | 171 | 31 | -7 | 14 | -1 | 359 |
| Australia | 135 | 6 | -21 | 29 | -13 | 167 |
| Italy | 115 | 17 | -21 | -4 | -24 | 188 |
| Taiwan | 101 | 103 | -54 | 6 | -27 | 61* |

\* 1987–92.

a Excluding dividends.

*Sources:* Morgan Stanley Capital International; IFC; Datastream.

## 7 Cross-border mergers and acquisitions, 1992

| | Value ($m) | Market share (%) | No. |
|---|---|---|---|
| **Country of buyer** | | | |
| UK | 16,595 | 27.9 | 305 |
| France | 13,674 | 23.0 | 147 |
| USA | 12,058 | 20.3 | 517 |
| Italy | 7,274 | 12.2 | 62 |
| Germany | 4,169 | 7.0 | 132 |
| Netherlands | 1,701 | 2.9 | 81 |
| Australia | 1,626 | 2.7 | 42 |
| Canada | 1,271 | 2.1 | 127 |
| Sweden | 1,068 | 1.8 | 72 |
| Total | 59,435 | 100.0 | 1,485 |
| **Country of seller** | | | |
| USA | 14,701 | 24.9 | 359 |
| Netherlands | 14,362 | 24.3 | 80 |
| Germany | 8,047 | 13.6 | 188 |
| France | 7,410 | 12.6 | 154 |
| UK | 7,378 | 12.5 | 248 |
| Australia | 2,164 | 3.7 | 49 |
| Canada | 2,155 | 3.7 | 133 |
| Sweden | 1,559 | 2.6 | 50 |
| Italy | 1,208 | 2.0 | 74 |
| Total | 58,984 | 100.0 | 1,335 |

*Source:* Securities Data Loop.

## 8 Highest foreign debt, 1991

| Country | $ bn |
| --- | --- |
| Brazil | 116.5 |
| Mexico | 101.7 |
| Indonesia | 73.6 |
| India | 71.6 |
| Ex-Soviet Union | 67.2 |
| Argentina | 63.7 |
| China | 60.8 |
| Poland | 52.5 |
| Turkey | 50.3 |
| Egypt | 40.6 |
| South Korea | 40.5 |
| Thailand | 35.8 |
| Nigeria | 34.5 |
| Venezuela | 34.4 |
| Philippines | 31.9 |
| Algeria | 28.6 |
| Portugal | 28.6 |
| Pakistan | 23.0 |
| Hungary | 22.7 |
| Malaysia | 21.4 |
| Morocco | 21.2 |
| Peru | 20.7 |
| Côte d'Ivoire | 18.8 |
| Chile | 17.9 |

*Source:* World Bank.

## 9 Share of national currencies in total identified official holdings of foreign exchange, 1983–92 (end year %)

| | 1983 | 1984 | 1985 | 1986 | 1987 | 1988 | 1989 | 1990 | 1991 | 1992 | Memorandum ECUs Treated Separately 1992 |
|---|---|---|---|---|---|---|---|---|---|---|---|
| **All countries** | | | | | | | | | | | |
| US dollar | 71.1 | 69.9 | 64.8 | 67.0 | 67.8 | 64.6 | 60.2 | 57.5 | 58.4 | 64.4 | 55.3 |
| Pound sterling | 2.5 | 2.9 | 3.0 | 2.5 | 2.4 | 2.7 | 2.7 | 3.4 | 3.6 | 3.2 | 3.1 |
| Deutsche mark | 11.7 | 12.6 | 15.1 | 14.6 | 14.4 | 15.6 | 19.0 | 18.6 | 16.5 | 13.0 | 12.5 |
| French franc | 0.8 | 0.8 | 0.9 | 0.8 | 0.8 | 1.0 | 1.4 | 2.3 | 2.8 | 2.5 | 2.4 |
| Swiss franc | 2.3 | 2.0 | 2.3 | 2.0 | 1.9 | 1.9 | 1.5 | 1.4 | 1.4 | 1.3 | 1.3 |
| Netherlands guilder | 0.8 | 0.7 | 1.0 | 1.1 | 1.2 | 1.1 | 1.1 | 1.1 | 1.1 | 0.7 | 0.7 |
| Japanese yen | 4.9 | 5.8 | 8.0 | 7.8 | 7.5 | 7.7 | 7.7 | 8.8 | 9.4 | 8.1 | 7.8 |
| **Industrial countries** | | | | | | | | | | | |
| US dollar | 77.2 | 73.5 | 65.2 | 69.4 | 71.4 | 67.7 | 59.6 | 56.0 | 55.8 | 64.9 | 49.9 |
| Pound sterling | 0.7 | 1.4 | 1.8 | 1.3 | 1.1 | 1.5 | 1.4 | 1.9 | 2.0 | 2.3 | 2.2 |
| Deutsche mark | 13.0 | 15.1 | 19.5 | 16.7 | 15.9 | 17.3 | 22.5 | 21.9 | 20.0 | 14.4 | 13.5 |
| French franc | 0.0 | 0.1 | 0.1 | 0.1 | 0.4 | 0.7 | 1.2 | 2.5 | 3.2 | 3.0 | 2.8 |
| Swiss franc | 1.5 | 1.5 | 2.1 | 1.7 | 1.6 | 1.7 | 1.1 | 1.1 | 0.8 | 0.6 | 0.5 |
| Netherlands guilder | 0.5 | 0.6 | 1.0 | 1.1 | 1.3 | 1.1 | 1.2 | 1.3 | 1.2 | 0.5 | 0.5 |
| Japanese yen | 5.1 | 6.3 | 8.9 | 8.3 | 7.1 | 7.0 | 8.1 | 9.6 | 10.4 | 7.4 | 7.0 |

*Source:* IMF Annual Reports.

## 10 Overview of the world economy[a], 1989–92
**(Annual % change unless otherwise indicated)**

|  | 1989 | 1990 | 1991 | 1992 |
|---|---|---|---|---|
| **World output** | **3.3** | **2.0** | **0.6** | **1.8** |
| Industrial countries | 3.2 | 2.1 | 0.2 | 1.5 |
| USA | 2.5 | 0.8 | −1.2 | 2.1 |
| Japan | 4.7 | 4.8 | 4.0 | 1.3 |
| Germany | 3.4 | 5.1 | 1.0 | 2.0 |
| France | 4.1 | 2.2 | 1.1 | 1.8 |
| Italy | 2.9 | 2.1 | 1.3 | 0.9 |
| UK | 2.1 | 0.5 | −2.2 | −0.6 |
| Canada | 2.3 | −0.5 | −1.7 | 0.9 |
| Seven countries above | 3.1 | 2.0 | 0.2 | 1.6 |
| Other industrial countries | 3.8 | 2.7 | 0.6 | 0.8 |
| *Memorandum* |  |  |  |  |
| European Community | 3.4 | 2.8 | 0.7 | 1.1 |
| Western Germany | 3.4 | 5.1 | 3.7 | 1.5 |
| Developing countries | 4.0 | 3.7 | 4.2 | 6.1 |
| Africa | 3.7 | 1.9 | 1.5 | 0.9 |
| Asia | 5.5 | 5.7 | 5.8 | 7.9 |
| Middle East and Europe | 2.9 | 3.9 | 2.1 | 9.9 |
| Western Hemisphere | 1.7 | 0.4 | 3.1 | 2.3 |
| Countries in transition | 1.9 | −3.6 | −10.1 | −15.5 |
| Central and Eastern Europe[b] | 0.2 | −7.4 | −13.5 | −7.5 |
| Former USSR | 2.5 | −2.2 | −9.0 | −18.5 |
| **World trade volume** | **7.0** | **4.4** | **2.3** | **4.2** |
| Industrial country import volume | 7.4 | 4.6 | 2.4 | 4.0 |
| Developing country import volume | 8.7 | 7.3 | 9.1 | 10.2 |
| **Commodity prices** | **21.5** | **28.2** | **−17.0** | **−0.5** |
| Oil[c] (*in US$ a barrel*) | 17.19 | 22.05 | 18.30 | 18.20 |
| Nonfuel[d] | −0.5 | −7.7 | −4.5 | −0.1 |
| **Consumer prices** |  |  |  |  |
| Industrial countries | 4.6 | 5.2 | 4.5 | 3.2 |
| Developing countries | 61.9 | 65.4 | 35.7 | 8.7 |
| Countries in transition | 27.6 | 32.4 | 100.5 | 776.2 |
| Central and Eastern Europe[b] | 135.5 | 158.8 | 119.4 | 196.6 |
| Former USSR | 2.3 | 5.4 | 94.7 | 1,201.8 |
| **Six-month LIBOR** (%)[e] |  |  |  |  |
| On US dollar deposits | 9.3 | 8.4 | 6.1 | 3.9 |
| On Japanese yen deposits | 5.5 | 7.8 | 7.2 | 4.3 |
| On Deutsche mark deposits | 7.2 | 8.8 | 9.4 | 9.4 |

a Country group composites for output and inflation are based on individual country estimates weighted by purchasing power parity (PPP) values of their respective GDPs.

b The countries in Central and Eastern Europe comprise Albania, Bulgaria, the Czech Republic, Hungary, Poland, Romania, the Slovak Republic, as well as Croatia, Slovenia, and the other republics of the former Socialist Federal Republic of Yugoslavia.

c Simple average of the US dollar spot prices of UK Brent, Dubai, and Alaska North Slope crude oil.

d In US dollars; based on world export weights.

e London interbank offered rate.

## 11 World gold production[a], 1953–92 (tonnes)

| Country | 1953 | 1970 | 1980 | 1987 | 1988 | 1989 | 1990 | 1991 | 1992 |
|---|---|---|---|---|---|---|---|---|---|
| South Africa | 371 | 1,000 | 675 | 607 | 621 | 608 | 605 | 601 | 614 |
| % share of world gold production | 49.1 | 78.6 | 70.2 | 43.8 | 40.0 | 36.1 | 34.7 | 33.7 | 33.4 |
| USA | 61 | 54 | 31 | 155 | 201 | 266 | 294 | 294 | 322 |
| Australia | 33 | 20 | 17 | 111 | 157 | 204 | 243 | 236 | 240 |
| Canada | 126 | 75 | 52 | 117 | 135 | 160 | 167 | 177 | 157 |
| Brazil | 4 | 9 | 35 | 85 | 102 | 101 | 84 | 79 | 71 |
| Papua New Guinea | 0 | 1 | 14 | 34 | 37 | 34 | 34 | 61 | 71 |
| Chile | 4 | 2 | 9 | 23 | 27 | 29 | 33 | 33 | 40 |
| Colombia | 14 | 7 | 17 | 33 | 33 | 32 | 33 | 31 | 30 |
| Philippines | 15 | 19 | 22 | 40 | 39 | 38 | 37 | 31 | 27 |
| Ghana | 23 | 22 | 11 | 12 | 12 | 15 | 17 | 27 | 34 |
| Other countries[a] | 104 | 64 | 79 | 169 | 188 | 194 | 197 | 207 | 228 |
| **Western world total** | **755** | **1,273** | **962** | **1,386** | **1,552** | **1,681** | **1,744** | **1,782** | **1,840** |
| **Memorandum items** | | | | | | | | | |
| (annual averages, US$/oz) | | | | | | | | | |
| Market price of gold: | | | | | | | | | |
| in current US$ | 35 | 36 | 615 | 447 | 437 | 381 | 384 | 362 | 344 |
| in constant US$[b] | 35 | 25 | 200 | 105 | 99 | 82 | 79 | 71 | 66 |

a Excluding the former Soviet Union, China and some minor producers.
b Deflated by the US consumer price index (1953 = 100).
*Sources:* Consolidated Gold Fields (London); Gold Fields Mineral Services (London).

**12 Domestic and international markets for commercial paper and medium-term notes, amounts outstanding at end-year, in billions of US dollars^a, 1986–92**

| | Market opening | 1986 | 1987 | 1988 | 1989 | 1990 | 1991 | 1992 |
|---|---|---|---|---|---|---|---|---|
| Commercial paper markets | | | | | | | | |
| USA | pre-1960 | 326.1 | 373.6 | 451.8 | 523.9 | 557.8 | 528.1 | 545.1 |
| Japan | end-1987 | | 13.8 | 73.8 | 91.1 | 117.3 | 99.0 | 98.1 |
| France | end-1985 | 3.7 | 7.6 | 10.4 | 22.3 | 31.0 | 30.8 | 31.6 |
| Spain^b | 1982 | 6.3 | 4.3 | 6.3 | 8.3 | 26.1 | 28.4 | 29.3 |
| Canada | pre-1960 | 11.9 | 14.9 | 21.0 | 25.0 | 26.6 | 27.4 | 24.5 |
| Sweden | 1983 | 3.7 | 7.8 | 9.5 | 15.9 | 23.1 | 24.0 | 16.6 |
| Australia^c | mid-1970s | 4.1 | 7.5 | 7.9 | 11.1 | 10.9 | 12.3 | 13.8 |
| Germany | early 1991 | | | | | | 5.4 | 10.2 |
| UK | 1986 | 0.8 | 3.8 | 5.7 | 5.7 | 7.4 | 6.9 | 5.8 |
| Total domestic | | 358.1 | 439.8 | 595.0 | 711.7 | 814.0 | 774.5 | 784.9 |
| | | | | | | | | |
| Euro commercial paper | mid-1980s | 13.9 | 33.3 | 53.2 | 58.5 | 70.3 | 79.6 | 78.7 |
| Other short-term Euro notes | early 1980s | 15.1 | 16.9 | 13.5 | 11.1 | 19.1 | 26.8 | 37.0 |
| Total | | 387.1 | 490.0 | 661.7 | 781.3 | 903.4 | 880.9 | 900.6 |
| | | | | | | | | |
| Medium-term note markets | | | | | | | | |
| USA | early 1970s | 35.0^d | 50.0^d | 65.0^d | 76.0 | 100.0 | 142.3 | 175.7 |
| UK | mid-1990 | | | | | 0.7 | 1.9 | 4.9 |
| | | | | | | | | |
| Euro medium-term notes | mid-1980s | 0.4 | 2.6 | 5.6 | 9.6 | 21.9 | 38.5 | 61.1 |

a Converted at current exchange rates.   b Up to 1991, non-financial institutions only.   c Up to 1991, mid-year data.   d Estimate.
*Sources*: Euroclear and national authorities.

# 13 The expansion of selected financial derivative markets, 1986–91 (notional principal amounts, $bn[a])

| Instrument | 1986 | 1987 | 1988 | 1989 | 1990 | 1991 |
|---|---|---|---|---|---|---|
| **Exchange-traded instruments** | 583 | 724 | 1,300 | 1,762 | 2,284 | 3,518 |
| Interest rate options & futures | 516 | 609 | 1,174 | 1,588 | 2,054 | 3,231 |
| Currency options & futures | 49 | 74 | 60 | 66 | 72 | 77 |
| Stock index options & futures | 18 | 41 | 66 | 108 | 158 | 210 |
| **Over-the-counter instruments** | 500 | 867 | 1,330 | 2,402 | 3,451 | 4,080[b,c] |
| Interest rate swaps | 400[b] | 683 | 1,010 | 1,503 | 2,312 | 2,750[b,c] |
| Currency & interest/currency swaps[d] | 100[b] | 184 | 320 | 449 | 578 | 700[b,c] |
| Other[d,e] | – | – | | 450 | 561 | 630[b,c] |
| **Grand total** | 1,083 | 1,591 | 2,630 | 4,164 | 5,735 | 6,900[b,c] |
| **Memorandum items** | | | | | | |
| Ratio of grand total to: | | | | | | |
| International claims[f] of BIS reporting banks | 0.27 | 0.31 | 0.47 | 0.64 | 0.76 | 1.00[g] |
| OECD GDP | 0.10 | 0.13 | 0.19 | 0.29 | 0.35 | 0.40[g] |

a Amounts outstanding at year-end.  b Estimate.  c June.  d Adjusted for reporting of both currencies.  e Caps, collars, floors and swaptions.
f Cross-border and local foreign currency claims.  g Estimates on the basis of June figures.
*Sources:* Futures Industry Association; International Swap Dealers Association; various futures and options exchanges worldwide; BIS calculations.

## 14 Cross-border transactions in bonds and equities[a], 1970–90 (% of GDP)

| Country | 1970 | 1975 | 1980 | 1985 | 1990 |
|---------|------|------|------|------|------|
| USA | 2.8 | 4.2 | 9.3 | 36.4 | 92.5 |
| Japan | n.a. | 1.5 | 7.0 | 60.5 | 118.6 |
| Germany | 3.3 | 5.1 | 7.5 | 33.9 | 57.5 |
| France | n.a. | n.a. | 8.4[b] | 21.4 | 53.3 |
| Italy | n.a. | 0.9 | 1.1 | 4.0 | 26.7 |
| UK | n.a. | n.a. | n.a. | 367.5 | 690.1 |
| Canada | 5.7 | 3.3 | 9.6 | 26.7 | 63.8 |

[a] Gross purchases and sales of securities between residents and non-residents.    [b] 1982.
*Source:* National balance-of-payments data.

**15 Indicators of growth in the financial industry, 1970–89 (%)**

| Country | Share in total employment | | | Share in value added[a] | | |
|---|---|---|---|---|---|---|
| | 1970 | 1979 | 1989 | 1970 | 1979 | 1989 |
| USA | 3.8 | 4.2 | 4.8 | 4.1 | 4.5 | 5.7[b] |
| Japan | 2.6 | 2.8 | 3.4 | 4.5 | 4.9 | 5.6 |
| Germany | 2.3 | 2.8 | 3.1[c] | 3.1 | 4.2 | 5.0 |
| France | n.a. | 12.6[d] | 16.1[d] | 3.3 | 3.5 | 4.7 |
| Italy | 1.6 | 1.6 | 1.8 | 2.9 | 3.9 | 4.4 |
| UK[d] | 6.0[e] | 7.0 | 11.4 | 12.5 | 14.8 | 20.0 |
| Canada | n.a. | 4.8[d,f] | 5.2[d] | 1.9 | 1.8 | 2.3[b] |
| Australia[d] | 7.1 | 8.1 | 11.0[c] | 8.5 | 9.0 | 12.1 |
| Belgium | 3.2[g] | 3.4 | 4.1 | 3.2[g] | 4.2 | 5.9 |
| Finland | 2.4[h] | 2.5 | 3.1 | 3.1[h] | 3.0 | 3.9 |
| Netherlands | n.a. | 3.5 | 3.8 | 2.9 | 4.5 | 4.9[b] |
| Norway | 1.9 | 2.2 | 3.0 | 2.3 | 3.1 | 4.4 |
| Spain | n.a. | 2.2 | 2.5 | 3.5 | 5.7[i] | 6.5 |
| Sweden | n.a. | 1.7[i] | 2.0 | n.a. | 3.1[i] | 4.4 |
| Switzerland | 2.7 | 4.2 | 5.3 | 4.6 | 5.8[g] | 10.1[j] |

a GNP/GDP plus imputed bank service charge, at current prices (1980 prices for France).   b 1987.   c 1988.   d Including real estate and business services.   e 1971.   f 1983.   g 1975.   h 1976.   i 1980.   j 1985.

*Sources:* OECD; national data; BIS estimates.

## 16 Bank profit margins[a], 1980–92

| Country | 1980–82 | 1984–86 | 1989–90 | 1990 | 1991 | 1992 |
|---|---|---|---|---|---|---|
| USA[b,c] | 0.83 | 0.83 | 0.61 | 0.59 | 0.60 | 1.12 |
| Japan[b,c] | 0.40 | 0.46 | 0.40 | 0.33 | 0.31 | 0.22 |
| Germany[b] | 0.50 | 0.97 | 0.88 | 0.83 | 0.63 | 0.67 |
| France[b] | 0.34 | 0.21 | 0.33 | 0.31 | 0.39 | 0.29 |
| UK[b] | 1.04 | 1.05 | 0.28 | 0.59 | 0.35 | 0.29 |
| Canada[c] | 0.63 | 0.74 | 0.96 | 1.22 | 1.26 | 0.60 |
| Australia[c] | 1.41 | 1.33 | 1.20 | 0.94 | 1.07 | −0.25 |
| Finland | 0.49 | 0.55 | 0.22 | 0.21 | −0.49 | −1.67 |
| Netherlands | 0.31 | 0.66 | 0.59 | 0.53 | 0.59 | 0.61 |
| Norway | 0.63 | 0.75 | −0.43 | −1.02 | −3.77 | −1.22 |
| Spain[b] | 1.09 | 0.92 | 1.75 | 1.72 | 1.24 | 0.94 |
| Sweden[d] | 0.38 | 0.55 | 0.34 | 0.22 | −0.41 | −1.99 |
| Switzerland | 0.65 | 0.71 | 0.64 | 0.53 | 0.74 | 0.73 |

a Ratio of pre-tax profit to average total assets of commercial banks; the data are not fully comparable across countries.    b Large commercial banks.    c Fiscal years.    d A break in series in 1986 considerably raises profit margins in that and subsequent years in comparison with 1980–85.
Sources: For Australia, Reserve Bank of Australia; for other countries, OECD and BIS estimates.

## 17 **Big privatisation deals, internationally**

**Largest initial public offerings**

| | Date | Value, $bn |
|---|---|---|
| Nippon Telegraph and Telephone (Japan) | 1986 | 12.4 |
| BP (Britain) | 1987 | 9.5 |
| British Gas | 1986 | 7.8 |
| BT (Britain) | 1984 | 4.9 |
| British Steel | 1988 | 4.5 |
| Scottish Power | 1991 | 3.7 |
| Société Générale (France) | 1987 | 3.7 |
| Yacimientos Petroliferos Fiscales (Argentina) | 1993 | 3.0 |
| National Power (Britain) | 1991 | 2.3 |
| Telefonos de Mexico | 1991 | 2.2 |

**Largest single private sales**

| | | |
|---|---|---|
| Procordia (Sweden) | 1989 | 3.8 |
| Banamex (Mexico) | 1991 | 3.2 |
| Gas del Estado (Argentina) | 1992 | 3.2 |
| Bancomer (Mexico) | 1991 | 2.6 |
| Telecom of New Zealand | 1990 | 2.5 |
| CANTV (Venezuela) | 1991 | 1.9 |
| Telefonos de Mexico | 1990 | 1.8 |
| Usiminas (Brazil) | 1991 | 1.5 |
| Mexicana de Cobre | 1988 | 1.4 |
| ENTel (Argentina) | 1990 | 1.3 |

*Sources:* Privatisation International; company reports.